PROPERTY OF

FEDERAL EXPRESS

Customer Automation Support
3063 Airways Blvd. Bldg D Suite 3
Memphis, TN 38194-5512

COMPOSITE/STRUCTURED
DESIGN

COMPOSITE/STRUCTURED
DESIGN

Glenford J. Myers

Senior Staff Member, IBM Systems Research Institute
Lecturer in Computer Science, Polytechnic Institute of New York

VAN NOSTRAND REINHOLD COMPANY

NEW YORK   CINCINNATI   ATLANTA   DALLAS   SAN FRANCISCO
LONDON   TORONTO   MELBOURNE

Van Nostrand Reinhold Company Regional Offices:
New York Cincinnati Atlanta Dallas San Francisco

Van Nostrand Reinhold Company International Offices:
London Toronto Melbourne

Library of Congress Catalog Card Number: 78-3417
ISBN: 0-442-80584-5

Manufactured in the United States of America

Published by Van Nostrand Reinhold Company
135 West 50th Street, New York, N.Y. 10020

Published simultaneously in Canada by Van Nostrand Reinhold Ltd.

15 14 13 12 11 10 9 8 7

Library of Congress Cataloging in Publication Data
Myers, Glenford J., 1946–
    Composite/structured design.

    Includes bibliographies and index.
    1. Electronic digital computers—Programming.
2. Computer programs.   I. Title.
QA76.6.M89   1978b   001.6'42   78-3417
ISBN 0-442-80584-5

TO GLORIA

CONTENTS

CONTENTS

Contents

PREFACE

The 1970s will probably be known as the decade in which software considerations surpassed hardware considerations. Concerns about the reliability and economics of data processing systems are now largely focused on software rather than hardware. Software costs now greatly exceed hardware costs, and issues of the prior two decades (e.g., minimizing hardware costs and forcing the optimum usage of every machine) have taken a backseat to software issues such as unsatisfactory reliability, excessive cost, and schedule overruns. This change in priorities has led to the development of a collection of methods and ideas to improve the programming process. This book discusses one of these methods known as *composite design*.

Of these new methods and ideas (e.g., structured programming, chief programmer teams, code walkthroughs), composite design has probably received the least publicity. The reasons for this include the fact that there are no underlying mathematical theorems about composite design (making it unappealing to many academics), and the subject is too extensive to be explained in a trade journal article or a three-page "programming standard." On the other hand, practitioners of composite design often feel that it is the most valuable of the new techniques because it addresses the fundamental problems of designing cheaper, more reliable, and more extensible programs.

The subject of composite design began to receive broader attention in 1976. A sign of this was a three-hour session on the subject at the 1976 National Computer Conference in which the four major contributors to the area—Larry Constantine, Michael Jackson, Edward Yourdon, and myself—discussed their individual approaches. The session was one of the most heavily attended at the NCC.

One source of confusion in discussing this topic is that it is known by two names: composite design and structured design. I prefer the term "composite design" and will use it throughout the book because I know of at least six unrelated design methods that at one time or another have been called "structured design."

The purpose of this book is to give the programmer or systems analyst a set of objectives and methods to design the structure of medium- or large-sized programs. Although the book is oriented to the design of application programs, the ideas have also been used in the design of system software (e.g., operating systems, compilers) and microprograms.

Since I wrote a book on this subject in 1974, one might ask why I am writing another. The reasons are threefold: I have had the benefit of several more years of thought, experience in teaching the subject, and feedback through consultation with people who were using these ideas.

In my opinion every programmer, systems analyst, programming project manager, and computer science student should become thoroughly familiar with the ideas in this book, because the design of highly reliable, maintainable, and extensible programs is fundamental to the economics of computing systems. The book can be used for reference, self-study, or as a text in a professional development program or university course. The questions and problems at the end of most of the chapters enhance its use as a text. The problems should be solved when each chapter is studied because many of the concepts are difficult to grasp without "hands-on" experience. A course on the subject *must* include an actual design problem. The instructor should write a realistic specification for a program, have the students design the program (individually or in teams), and then critique the design. As a point of reference, I have frequently used the program illustrated in Chapter 12 as a homework problem. A problem of equivalent size is probably optimal (students spend an average of 15 hours to design the program in Chapter 12).

The 16 chapters in this book fall into three categories. The first six chapters define the goals; they discuss the objectives and measures of a well-designed program. Chapters 7 through 13 focus on the "how-to" aspects of design. In other words, given that we agree on the objectives and measures in the first six chapters, what thought-processes (decomposition techniques) can be used to achieve the desired results? The last three chapters discuss the implementation of composite design, including its relationships to programming languages and to other methodologies such as structured programming and programming teams.

I am grateful to the IBM Systems Research Institute for the support of my research, teaching, and consultation on this subject, and to the many students who provided me with valuable debates, feedback, and criticism of the ideas. I thank my colleague, R. Goldberg, for helpful suggestions on the book. I am also grateful to the many members in the PL/I and productivity projects of GUIDE International for their avid interest and to all others who have not only used composite design but have reported their experiences to me.

Glenford J. Myers
New York, New York
December 1976

1

On the Subject of Program Design

If one steps back and views the entire process of program development from beginning to end, it is rather surprising that the human race has been able to develop even a few successful computer applications. The input to the program development process is a short, ambiguous, and incomplete statement of requirements for some new sophisticated program or system. The result of the process is a string of perhaps millions of zero and one bits which instruct a set of electronic devices on how to perform as such a system.

With such a view of programming, people quickly recognized that mastering complexity was the key to successful software development. The concept of assemblers and assembly languages was an initial step toward this goal because it removed from the programmer the requirement to remember that one must code the bit string 011010 to compare the values of two registers. The concept of higher-level languages and their compilers was an even larger step because it allowed the programmer to work without being an expert on the details and idiosyncracies of the machine. After this step people began to recognize that programmers needed better methods and tools to manage complexity; therefore, such ideas as structured programming, code reading, and program development libraries arose.

Although these contributions have been valuable, they still leave a lot to be desired. For instance, if one took the world's most troublesome program (a well-known operating system) and entirely recoded it using a high-level language and the concept of structured programming, it is unlikely that the result would be much of an improvement. In other words, there is much more to the subject of complexity than simply attempting to minimize the local complexity of each part of a program. A much more important type of complexity is *global complexity:* the complexity of the overall structure of a program or system (i.e., the degree of association or interdependence among the major pieces of a program).

Since this book is about some solutions to the problem of global or structural complexity (understanding it, dealing with it, and minimizing it), it is helpful to discuss the problem before examining the solutions. Therefore, nine fundamental problems in the area of program design are briefly discussed below.

The structure of the typical program is never designed; rather, it is created in an ad hoc manner on the coding pad.

The implication of this is that we deal with many of our decisions backwards. Rather than deal with the structural aspects of a system first and the procedural aspects later, we tend to do the opposite. In other words, we make the mistake of making vital overall structural decisions while coding the program.

The blame for this falls on many individuals. For instance, data processing managers feel uncomfortable during the design process because they are unable to make such meaningless statements as "95% of our code is written" or "82% of the test cases have been executed." Because of the difficulty of quantifying design progress, many project managers tend to push the project through the design phase as quickly as possible. The education process is also partly to blame. Programmers and students are trained in such aspects of programming as programming languages, good programming style, standards, documentation techniques, and algorithms; however, this is usually with the exclusion of analysis and design methods.

Most programs cannot adapt to changing requirements and environments.

Here one must face a basic fact of data processing: programmers rarely write throw-away programs. Most programs tend to have long lives and are subjected to considerable change, yet program modification is usually an expensive and highly error-prone process. This implies that, over the long run, program extensibility or adaptability is a vital economic factor.

Programmers spend the majority of their time correcting their mistakes.

Moreover they never finish. Examinations of typical programming projects will show that, over the duration of the project, programmers spend over 50% of their working hours looking for and correcting their mistakes. The usual "solution" to this is remarkable. We try to solve the problem by rushing through the design process so that enough time is left at the end of the project to uncover the errors that were made because we rushed through the design process.

The problems caused by placing insufficient emphasis on design are graphically illustrated in Figure 1.1, which represents the errors found after a series of modifications of a large program. [1] Analysis and design errors represented 64% of the total errors but, more importantly, they were much more difficult to detect.

2

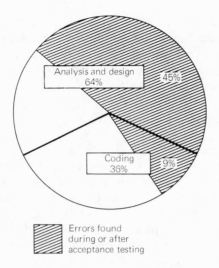

Analysis and design
64%

45%

Coding
36%

9%

Errors found
during or after
acceptance testing

Figure 1.1   Error sources and testing success

The development organization was able to detect 75% of their coding errors but only 30% of their design errors.

> *Software reliability, once the subject of many jokes, is now a life-and-death matter.*

Programming errors were once the subject of many hilarious stories in the press and trade journals. However, errors are no longer a laughing matter. There have been software errors in aerospace programs that have resulted in the failure of space missions. Software errors have put state lotteries out of business. Other errors have led to false arrests and, in a few cases, to deaths.

> *Despite a lot of supposed improvements in the programming process, the cost of producing software has not decreased significantly over the last 20 years.*

Although the cost of hardware has dropped dramatically, the cost of software has remained relatively stable. If one was to take an application that had been developed 20 years ago and attempt to develop the same application today, the labor cost would be approximately the same.

Technical design decisions are rarely objective.

It is unusual to see two program designers, who are debating alternatives, walk to the blackboard and attempt to evaluate their options by determining the effects each would have on reliability, complexity, cost, extensibility, and maintainability. More often than not, design decisions are based on group pressures ("the majority rules"), "old wives' tales" ("every program must have initialization, processing, and termination phases"), personal prejudices ("I like to do it this way"), and emotion ("do it my way or else").

We do not stand on the shoulders of others.

We tend to fabricate each new house from mud, grass, rough lumber, and prayer instead of from preassembled walls, window kits, and engineering know-how. It is rare to see a new program constructed from pieces of existing programs. Certainly no one will admit to having an easy solution to this problem. In part, it is a design problem in that the design of existing programs influences the chances that pieces of those programs can be reused. However, it is also a management and motivational problem in environments where programmers are measured on the number of statements they create. Furthermore, it is a documentation problem as it is necessary to readily locate existing parts of programs that may be appropriate to new applications.

A project of n programmers usually has n sets of objectives.

Typically we spend insufficient time establishing goals for what we are to produce. When we do not establish these goals and tradeoffs beforehand, they are often determined at a later point in an implicit and inconsistent fashion. For instance, programmer A's goal is maximizing speed at the cost of everything else; B's goal is minimizing cost at the sacrifice of everything else; and C's goal is producing fabulous documentation. The outcome of this three-programmer project is unpredictable.

The program design phases are regarded too informally.

How often have you seen a nebulous phase called "logic design" or "internal design" when there should have been measurable phases of system design, program structure design, data base or file design, module interface design, and module logic design? The advantage of more formality is that one can introduce additional measurable checkpoints, establish which methodologies will be used for which type of design, and attempt to use techniques to validate the quality of the design after each phase.

With these nine problems in mind, one could develop a set of off-hand solutions. For instance, the problems imply that more emphasis should be placed on design, extensibility, reliability, and cost. It might also seem that more objective design criteria are needed, and that the design process should be planned more intelligently. However, the broader solution to these problems is a need for a "science" or "culture" of software structure. In other words, what is required is set of "scientific" principles of system synthesis, system connectivity, and complexity control.

There is a shared recognition by others in the field that such a system of principles for software structure is necessary. "These problems are symptomatic of the lack of an adequate basis in the methodology, technology, and theory of information systems and/or a lack of disciplined application of the methodology and technology we do possess."[2] "The answer is that system designers must gradually develop a culture of system architecture similar to the one that exists today for the construction of houses and large buildings."[3] "If we *do* wish to develop standardized off-the-shelf software mechanisms, then we first need to study and understand the problems of systemic structure and element connectivity."[4] "Other parts of our operating systems are inextricably intertwined . . . They need not be if we had system design methodologies which would allow us to engineer into our implementation various safeguards to enforce elemental independence."[4]

Composite design is in no way a "science," but it is a step in this direction. Although composite design is not based on any known laws of nature or "theorems of composite design," it still can be considered as a set of engineering principles because it gives one a set of concepts, measurements, guidelines, and thought-processes related to understanding and designing program structures. As is the case with all types of engineering (e.g., circuit design, highway design, airplane design), the human being is still the vital part of the process because it is he or she that contributes ingenuity, creativity, and experience.

There are those who occasionally frown upon composite design because "it is not based on mathematical theorems as structured programming is." However, whether structured programming is actually based on mathematical fundamentals is a matter of interpretation. The "frowners" quote Bohm and Jacopini's theorem which shows that any flowchart program can be written using only sequential statements and IFTHENELSE and DOWHILE control constructs.[5] Note, however, that this theorem does not in any way imply that this is a good thing to do. One could develop an equally rigorous proof showing that any flowchart program could be written using sequential statements and IF-THENELSE and GOTO constructs. Structured programming advocates will also point to Ashcroft and Manna's rigorous algorithm[6] which removes the GOTOs from any flowchart program by introducing auxiliary boolean variables. Still, many people question the wisdom of this transformation.[7] Since we cannot use these as proof of the "goodness" of structured programming, we might turn to experimental results; however, there are not any. Therefore, the reasons that we openly accept structured programming are experience, intuition, and example; we *feel* (rightfully so) that structured programming does increase code readability and reduce logic complexity.

THE DESIGN PROCESSES

Before discussing the methodology of composite design, it is best to put it in perspective with relation to the overall software design process. The reason for this is that composite design is not a cure for all ills; it is only concerned with one particular aspect of software design. For instance, composite design will not help one gain a better understanding of end-user requirements nor will it help one write more readable source code.

The best way to understand the nature of composite design is to examine its inputs and outputs. Hopefully, all software projects begin with an analysis of the end-users' requirements. Since these requirements are usually contradictory, the next process is the establishment of measurable goals and objectives for the product, making tradeoffs among conflicting requirements when necessary. The next design process, called external design, results in the development of a precise and detailed external or user-oriented specification. That is, a specification describing the program's interactions with the outside world (e.g., its users) is established. It is this external specification that is the input to the composite design process.

Given a statement of what a program is to do, composite design is a methodology for designing the overall structure of that program. The output of this process is threefold. One output is the definition of the hierarchical module structure of the program. The second output is a definition of the function of each module in the program. The third output is an imprecise definition of all module interfaces ("imprecise" means that the information transmitted among modules is identified, but its precise structure, attributes, and so forth are left undefined).

Following this design process, one would expect to see two more design steps. The first, module interface design, is concerned with precisely defining the interfaces among all modules. The last design step, module logic design, is the designing and coding of the procedure or logic of each module.

If the product being developed is a *system* rather than a single program, there is another design process that must occur between the external design process and the use of composite design. This process, called system design, is the decomposition of the system into a set of individual subsystems or programs. Although some of the ideas of composite design are appropriate here and some people have claimed to have used composite design for this process, composite design does not appear to be directly applicable to system design. Therefore, when designing a system, as opposed to an individual program, the designer must first partition the system into distinct subsystems or programs. Then the methodology of composite design can be used to produce the structure of these individual pieces.

ANNOTATED BIBLIOGRAPHY

The following describes the known books, papers, articles, and experience reports that directly discuss some aspect of composite design. The list is in chronological order.

L. L. Constantine, "The Programming Profession, Programming Theory, and Programming Education," *Computers and Automation*, 17(2), 1968, 14–19.

> This short essay mentions, almost in passing, the key goals of composite/structured design: minimizing module interconnections and maximizing the "cohesiveness" of module content. Many of the programming profession problems discussed in this essay are still applicable today.

L. L. Constantine, "Segmentation and Design Strategies for Modular Programs," in T. O. Barnett and L. L. Constantine, Eds., *Modular Programming: Proceedings of a National Symposium*. Cambridge, Mass.: Information and Systems Institute, 1968, 23–42.

> This is the pioneering paper in the area. It introduces some of the measures of module definition and interconnection and stresses that structural design must be done before procedural design. This symposium reprint has been out of print for many years and is difficult to find.

G. J. Myers, "Composite Design: The Design of Modular Programs," TR–00.2406, IBM Poughkeepsie Laboratory, Poughkeepsie, N. Y., 1973.

> This report was the first widely-distributed (for example, it was translated into Japanese) comprehensive treatment of the subject. Some of the terminology and concepts are now obsolete.

G. J. Myers, "Characteristics of Composite Design," *DATAMATION*, 19(9), 1973, 100–102.

> This short article summarizes the major goals of composite design: maximizing module strength and minimizing module coupling.

G. J. Myers, "A Model for Predicting Program Change," TR-00.2491, IBM Poughkeepsie Laboratory, Poughkeepsie, N.Y., 1973.

> This report describes an experimental mathematical model of program structures based on the measures of composite design. The research effort was later abandoned because of the inability to collect the necessary data to validate the model.

W. P. Stevens, G. J. Myers, and L. L. Constantine, "Structured Design," *IBM Systems Journal*, 13(2), 1974, 115–139.

> A somewhat obsolete, and somewhat confusing, introduction to the subject.

G. J. Myers, "Designing Structured Programs Using Composite Design," *Proceedings of the 38th Meeting of GUIDE International*. New York: GUIDE International Corp., 1974, 275–277.

> This paper is a very brief overview of the subject.

G. J. Myers, "Designing Structured Programs Using Composite Design," *Proceedings of Share XLIII.* New York: SHARE Inc., 1974, 793–815.

This paper consists of a very brief six-page introduction and copies of 39 35mm slides on the subject.

L. Milligan and P. Fandel, "PL/I Structured Programming Case Study," *Proceedings of the 39th Meeting of GUIDE International.* New York: GUIDE International Corp., 1974, 585–605.

Composite design is reviewed, using a print-billing-notice program as an example.

Structured Programming Independent Study Program: Textbook. SR20–7149, IBM Corp., Poughkeepsie, N. Y., 1974.

Assignment six in this manual illustrates the use of one of the decomposition methods of composite design on two small programs.

G. J. Myers, *Reliable Software Through Composite Design.* New York: Petrocelli/Charter, 1975.

This is the first book on the subject of composite design. It includes a chapter describing a method to optimize program performance in a paging system through the proper physical organization of modules.

R. C. Cocking, "An Experiment with Composite Design," TR–00.2643, IBM Poughkeepsie Laboratory, Poughkeepsie, N.Y., 1975.

This experience report discusses the successful use of composite design on a 7100–statement documentation analysis program. Three positive effects are noted: the project finished on schedule, programmer productivity was high, and the program was found to be easy to change.

G. J. Myers, "Composite Design: A Method for Top-Down Program Design," *ACPA–V Proceedings.* Kensington, Md: ACPA, 1975, 42–45.

This paper is a more comprehensive overview of the concepts of composite design.

G. J. Myers, "Composite Design: A Method for Top-Down Program Design," *Proceedings of the 41st Meeting of GUIDE International.* New York: GUIDE International Corp., 1975, 641–646.

Same as the previous paper.

S. Bonner, "Educating Experienced Programmers in the Programmer Productivity Techniques," *Proceedings of the 41st Meeting of GUIDE International.* New York: GUIDE International Corp., 1975, 470–478.

Some considerations in implementing composite design in a data processing organization are discussed, including some advice on education and reasons why one organization switched from COBOL to PL/I.

M. Jackson, *Principles of Program Design*. London: Academic Press, 1975.

Jackson's book is a detailed description of his decomposition technique (discussed in Chapter 11 of this book). The technique is focused upon structuring a program according to the structure of its input and output data.

J. G. Rogers, "Structured Programming for Virtual Storage Systems," *IBM Systems Journal*, 14(4), 1975, 385–406.

This paper discusses the relationships of composite design and structured programming to efficiency in virtual storage environments. Considerations peculiar to IBM's major COBOL, FORTRAN, and PL/I compilers are also discussed.

E. Yourdon and L. L. Constantine, *Structured Design*. New York: Yourdon, Inc., 1975.

This is the second major work on composite/structured design. It offers a somewhat different perspective on the subject. The book also discusses more "exotic" concepts such as the use of coroutines.

E. Yourdon, *How to Manage Structured Programming*. New York: Yourdon, Inc., 1976.

Chapter 4 contains an overview of structured design and a few pages of advice to project managers on common problems encountered in putting the ideas into practice.

J. F. Stay, "HIPO and Integrated Program Design," *IBM Systems Journal*, 15(2), 1976, 143–154.

This is a brief discussion of the integration of composite design and HIPO (hierarchy plus input-process-output) diagrams.

K. T. deLavigne, "Basic Program Design—The Jackson Way: An Example," TR–00.2762, IBM Poughkeepsie Laboratory, Poughkeepsie, N. Y., 1976.

This report illustrates Jackson's decomposition technique. Unfortunately the example is too small and simple to be convincing.

L. Milligan, "Structured Programming—The After Effects," *Proceedings of the 42nd Meeting of GUIDE International*. New York: GUIDE International Corp., 1976, 601–612.

This paper discusses a cross-reference system being developed to allow an organization with a large inventory of "composite-designed" modules to search for modules that might be useful in future applications. Modules are given an "index of reuse" based, in part, on their module strength and coupling.

G. J. Myers, *Software Reliability: Principles and Practices*. New York: Wiley-Interscience, 1976.

Chapter 6 discusses composite design and illustrates its use on the design of a linkage editor/loader.

G. J. Myers, "Composite Design Facilities of Six Programming Languages," *IBM Systems Journal*, 15(3), 1976, 212–224.

This paper examines the relationships between composite design and six widely used programming languages, pointing out potential pitfalls in the languages. Language extensions that enhance the full potential of composite design are also suggested.

REFERENCES

1. B. W. Boehm, R. K. McClean, and D. B. Urfrig, "Some Experiences with Automated Aids to the Design of Large-Scale Reliable Software," *IEEE Transactions on Software Engineering*, SE–1(1), 1975, 125–133.
2. I. L. Auerbach, "Need for an Information Systems Theory," in H. Zemanek, Ed., *The Skyline of Information Processing*. Amsterdam: North-Holland, 1972, 9–21.
3. F. M. Haney, "What it Takes to Make MAC, MIS, and ABM Fly," *DATAMATION*, 20(6), 1974, 168–169.
4. M. J. Spier, "A Critical Look at the State of Our Science," *Operating Systems Review*, 8(2), 1974, 9–15.
5. C. Bohm and G. Jacopini, "Flow Diagrams, Turing Machines, and Languages with Only Two Formation Rules," *Communications of the ACM*, 9(5), 1966, 366–371.
6. E. Ashcroft and Z. Manna, "The Translation of 'GO TO' Programs to 'WHILE' Programs," *Proceedings of the 1971 IFIP Congress*, Booklet TA–2. Amsterdam: North-Holland, 1971, 147–152.
7. D. E. Knuth, "Structured Programming with GO TO Statements," *Computing Surveys*, 6(4), 1974, 261–301.

2

Definitions and Notation

Part of the methodology of composite design is a collection of notation for describing program structures and a substantial set of new terminology. The working vocabulary of the composite design practitioner includes such terms as *fan-in, informational strength, stamp coupling, predictable module,* and *module context.* In fact, in the beginning, composite design may appear to be simply an adventure in the English language.

This terminology is unfortunate from one point of view since the computing industry already has an overabundance of new words, misused words, and acronyms. However, our language for describing program structure is rather weak, and much of this terminology fills this gap by describing structural relationships and conditions within programs. The terminology also serves as a communications shorthand. For instance, rather than repeatedly referring to a certain kind of module as "a module that performs a class of functions where, upon each invocation of the module, one of these functions is explicitly selected by the calling module," one can just refer to it as a *logical-strength module.* Furthermore, it should be remembered that it is the concepts defined by the terminology, not the terminology itself, that are important.

STRUCTURAL TERMINOLOGY

The primary unit of program structure is called a *module.* A module is any collection of executable program statements meeting all of the following criteria: 1) it is a closed subroutine, 2) it can be called from any other module in the program, and 3) it has the potential of being independently compiled. Note that the last two criteria do not imply that for something to be a module it must be called from every other module and be independently compiled. Rather, these criteria imply that a module must have the "potential" of being called from any module and the "possibility" of separate compilation. Hence, entities such as PL/I external procedures and functions; FORTRAN subroutine subprograms

11

and function subprograms; COBOL subprograms; and APL functions meet the definition of a module. However, such entities as imbedded or included program segments, PL/I internal procedures, and COBOL performed paragraphs are not modules because they violate one or more of the criteria.

Another set of terms is needed to describe hierarchical control relationships among modules. Module B is said to be *subordinate* to module A if B is called by A or if B is called by a subordinate of A. Module B is said to be *immediately subordinate* to module A if B is called by A. In a similar fashion, module A is *superordinate* to module B if A calls B or if A calls a superordinate of B. Module A is *immediately superordinate* to module B if A calls B.

Two additional structural terms are *fan-in* and *fan-out.* The fan-in of a module is the number of distinct modules that call this module (i.e., the number of modules that are immediately superordinate to this module). The fan-out of a module is the number of distinct modules that are called by this module (the number of immediately subordinate modules). Note that it is not always the case that the fan-out of a module is equal to the number of call statements in that module.*

FUNCTION, LOGIC, AND CONTEXT

When we speak of a module, we can describe it by its function, its logic, or its context. A module's *function* defines *what* the module does. A module's *logic* describes *how* the module performs its function or, in other words, the internal algorithm or procedure of the module. A module's *context* describes a particular usage of a module. The reason for distinguishing among these three terms is that when using composite design a module is described by naming its function. Therefore, composite design is most directly concerned with module function and only indirectly concerned with module logic and context.

Since failing to distinguish properly between these three terms is a common problem in the use of composite design, a few simple examples might be helpful. Consider the analogy of a clock on a wall. The function of a clock is to display the current time of day. However, one can implement the logic of the clock in many ways. A motor could be used to tie the clock to the 60 cycle per second electrical supply. A crystal oscillator is a second alternative to implement the clock's logic. Other alternatives are using the energy in a wound spring or a set of weights, using a radio receiver tuned to a special time-broadcast, or even connecting the clock to a sundial on the roof. Although the logic of these alternatives is considerably different, the function of the clock remains the same.

Besides describing the clock in terms of function and logic, we can also examine the contexts in which the clock is used. Of course the obvious context

---

*The term "call statement" will always be used in a generic language-independent sense, meaning a statement or expression that transfers control from one module to another.

is to determine the time of day; however, another alternative might be glancing at the second-hand to obtain a uniformly distributed, random number from 1 to 60. If, for some reason, a memory lapse has caused us to forget the number between five and seven, we could also use the clock in another context—finding the answer six.

A second example illustrating the distinction among function, logic, and context is a square-root subroutine. The function of a square-root module is to compute the square-root of a number. Again there are many different alternatives in devising the logic of the module such as using a table or computing a logarithm. One can also use this single-function module in many contexts to compute such factors as the square-root of the speed of light, the square-root of the mass of a particle, or any number smaller than Z, given that Z is greater than one.

A third example that delineates a difference between function and logic is the design of a COBOL compiler. The "top" module (initial point of entry) of the compiler probably performs the function "compile a COBOL program." If, for some reason, one decided to design the entire compiler as one module, the function and logic of this module would be quite similar. However, if the designer was a little wiser and decided to construct the compiler as a collection of 133 modules, then even though the function of the top module would still be "compile a COBOL program," the logic of this module would be considerably different than before. Therefore, the function of a module includes the effects of all modules that are subordinate to that module, but the logic of the module does not. Hence, we can say: *The function of a module is "a function of" the module's logic and the functions of all immediately subordinate modules.*

When describing modules, several rules should be followed. A module should be described by its function, not its logic or contexts. For instance the term "main control module" will never be used because it is a description of logic, not function. When defining a function, use a *verb/object* form; that is, describe a module as doing something (or a set of things) to something. Examples of this type of description are "compile a COBOL program," "obtain the next input transaction," "sort the R205 file by specified key field," "remove duplicates from the symbol table and condense it," and "explode the bill-of-material." Finally, when using the verb/object form, avoid tempting but completely meaningless verbs. For instance, such function descriptions as "process the master file record," "handle the command parameters," and "manage the summary table" are completely meaningless. Verbs of this nature must be avoided.

NOTATION

Associated with composite design is a set of graphical notation. The aim of this notation is to describe the static, hierarchical structure of a program without describing its procedure (execution flow).

Figure 2.1 illustrates the basic symbols. The rectangle represents a module.

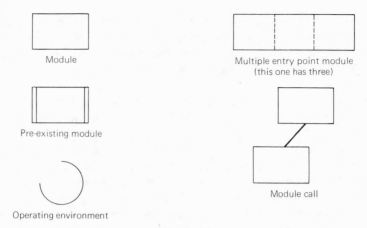

Figure 2.1 The basic symbols

Within the rectangle one places either the symbolic name of the module or its verb/object function description—the latter being preferable. The preexisting-module symbol denotes an existing module that is being incorporated into a program. Because preexisting modules are treated as "black boxes," any subordinates of preexisting modules are usually excluded from the diagram. The three-quarter circle is optionally used to denote a function in the host software system (e.g., operating system, data base management system). For instance, it is often desirable in an application program to show which modules "call" the operating environment for input/output services.

Lines between these symbols represent calls. The convention is that a line connected to the bottom edge of a symbol is a call from that module to some other module, and a line connected to the top edge is a call to that module from some other module.

A rectangle with vertical, dashed lines in its midst is a module with multiple entry points. Lines entering the top edge of this symbol should be placed to indicate the entry point called, but lines leaving the bottom edge of this symbol are not assumed to be associated with any particular entry point.

An important part of the notation is a description of the information being transmitted along module interfaces. Figure 2.2 illustrates the notation for describing interfaces. For instance, from Figure 2.2 one can deduce that there is a call statement in module A, and it might appear as

CALL B (CODE,DATE,STAB)
or CALL 'B' USING CODE,DATE,STAB.*

---

*Figure 2.2 is atypical in that it presumably lists actual argument names. When one uses the notation in the design process, the interface lists are more descriptive.

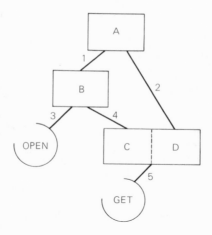

	IN	OUT
1	CODE, DATE	STAB
2	STAB	STAB, ERROR
3	FNAME	—
4	STAB, DATE	VALID
5	—	RECORD

Figure 2.2   Interface definitions

It should also be noted that Figure 2.2 distinguishes between input and output data. An input datum is something whose value is significant upon entry. An output datum is something whose value is assigned or changed (or potentially assigned or changed) between the times of entry and return. Note, as in interface 2|, that an item can be both an input and output. Finally, interface data are always described from the calling module's point of view.

When using the graphical notation, a few basic rules to follow are that the entire diagram for a program should appear on a single piece of paper which, for a large program, might cover an entire wall; for ease of readability a module should appear only once in the diagram; and each interface should be given a unique interface number. If, for some reason, the diagram must be spread over multiple pages, the dashed box in Figure 2.3 is used to denote a module that appears, along with its subordinate modules, on another page. If the diagram becomes overly complex because of many crossing interface lines, two interface connectors containing some arbitrary letter can be used to connect two widely separated modules. Connectors should be used sparingly because they make the diagram more difficult to follow. When an interface connector is used, the interface number should appear at both locations of the connector. (Interface connectors are used in Figure 12.14 in Chapter 12.)

15

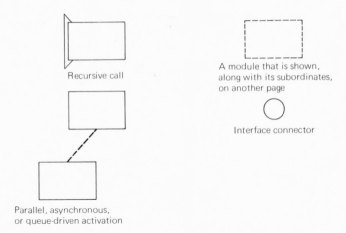

Recursive call

Parallel, asynchronous,
or queue-driven activation

A module that is shown,
along with its subordinates,
on another page

Interface connector

Figure 2.3   Auxiliary symbols

INTERFACE CHART			Program:		Date:	Page ___ of ___		
Inter-face no.	Calling module	Called module	IN	OUT	Coup-ling	Type of call[1]	Prob. of call[2]

1: I = Iterative, N = Not iterative
2: Probability that when the calling module is entered, it will invoke the called module.

Figure 2.4   Module interface form

In large projects it may be desirable to define interfaces on preprinted forms. One such form is shown in Figure 2.4. The meaning of the COUPLING column will be obvious after reading Chapter 5; it describes the type of coupling between the two modules. The last two columns are not of interest at this point; they provide information to an algorithm that can be used to optimize the packaging of a program in a virtual storage system.[1]

Notational Style

Several stylistic points about the notation are worth mentioning. The position of a module on the page has no direct bearing on its position within the program structure; however, where possible, it is desirable to position a module's subordinates below the module in the diagram. Likewise, the horizontal relationship among a module's subordinates has no defined meaning, but if a module consistently calls its subordinates in the order A, then B, then C, it is appropriate to order the modules this way (left to right) in the diagram.

Normally, when one module calls another, only one line appears between the modules regardless of the number of distinct call statements appearing in the calling module. However, there are situations where a module A might call module B in several different contexts implying that a single interface definition will not suffice. In this case it is appropriate to draw multiple interface lines from A to B.

HIPO DIAGRAMS

For those readers familiar with HIPO (hierarchy plus input-process-output) diagrams[2], a discussion is in order because the previous notation seems contradictory to, and redundant with, HIPO documentation.

HIPO documentation includes two types of diagrams: an input-process-output chart showing the input data, output data, and processing steps for an individual function; and a "visual table of contents" (VTOC), a tree-like hierarchy of boxes presumably showing the structure of the program and serving as an index to the individual function charts. It is the latter diagram that is inconsistent and redundant with the notation of the previous section.

The recommendation is that if HIPO documentation is used in conjunction with composite design, then the composite design structural notation should be used instead of, and as a replacement for, the HIPO VTOC diagram. The rationale for this is that the VTOC is intended to be a tree structure (a box has only one parent), yet most programs, particularly well-designed programs, are not tree structures. Hence, this leads one to repeat an individual module in multiple places in the diagram. Not only does such a diagram not accurately depict the program's true structure, but it makes the program look larger than it actually is, and it makes finding all of a module's immediate superordinates a more difficult task.

Another reason for using the composite design structural notation is that the VTOC is often a conceptual picture of the program rather than an actual picture. That is, a VTOC is often an "artist's conception" of the structure of the program. VTOC's are often drawn for convenience rather than accuracy (e.g., "These functions are not shown as they appear in the physical structure of the program" [2] page 29).

Besides the above reasons, it should also be noted that the VTOC contains no interface information, so one must leaf through the individual function charts to find it. However, it is important to have interface information readily at hand when examining a program structure because a terse description of a module's function is usually not completely clear until one can see the function's input and output data.

A final justification for not using the HIPO VTOC diagram in this instance is that since input-process-output charts lump all of a module's inputs and outputs together, they do not clearly distinguish among which "input" data are being transmitted to a module from its caller, which data are being received from its subordinates, and which data are obtained from input operations. Likewise, they do not distinguish among which "output" data are transmitted to the module's caller, which data are transmitted to its subordinates, and which data are written in I/O operations.

REFERENCES

1. G. J. Myers, *Reliable Software Through Composite Design*. New York: Petrocelli/ Charter, 1975.
2. *HIPO—A Design Aid and Documentation Technique*. GC20–1851, IBM Corp., White Plains, N. Y., 1974.

EXERCISES

1. Under what conditions is the fan-out of a module less than the number of call statements in the module?

2. Under what conditions is the fan-out of a module greater than the number of call statements in the module?

3. Can a module be subordinate and/or superordinate to itself?

4. Compile a list of meaningless verbs that should be avoided when defining module function.

5. Take an existing program and describe the function, logic, and context of each module.

6. Although a module's function and context are often similar, what is the danger of defining a module by its context rather than by its function?

7. Read the program below and describe it using the notation (modules, module relationships, and interfaces). The program is not intended to make any sense. Also it is not coded in any particular programming language although it resembles PL/I. Assume the argument-transmission method is that of PL/I, COBOL, and FORTRAN (transmission by reference). Hint: the problem is harder than it first appears to be.

```
REPORT: PROCEDURE          ARB: PROCEDURE(N,M)
CALL ARB (A,B)             Z=N+17
CALL LOCATE (X)            CALL ZEBRA (Z)
END                        M=Z
                           END

ZEBRA: PROCEDURE (Z)
Z=Z+4                      LOCATE: PROCEDURE (X)
RETURN                     ELE=X
FORT: ENTRY (XYZ)          CALL FORT (X)
XYZ=XYZ+1                  CALL ARB (X,L)
END                        CALL ZERO (L)
                           END

ZERO: PROCEDURE (ALAN)
ALAN=ALAN/2
CALL ZERO (ALAN)
X=TIME(T) /*TIME IS AN OPERATING SYSTEM FUNCTION THAT
              RETURNS THE TIME OF DAY*/
END
```

8. In the program above, what is the fan-in and fan-out of LOCATE?

9. What modules are superordinate to ZERO?

10. What modules are immediately subordinate to REPORT?

11. What is the meaning of the following diagram?

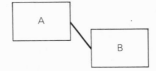

3

Underpinnings of a Good Design

As a starting point in solving some of the problems discussed in Chapter 1, we should consider the attributes that well-structured programs have and how they differ from those of programs of poor or mediocre structure. The major visible difference between good and poor program structures seems to be *complexity;* therefore, attention can be focused on three universal means of reducing complexity in any type of system (e.g., a computer program, a human organization, a biological system, an automobile): 1) partitioning the system into parts having identifiable and understandable boundaries, 2) representing the system as a hierarchy, and 3) maximizing the independence among the parts of the system.

PARTITIONING

The act of partitioning a program into individual components can reduce its complexity to some degree. For instance, a study of 120 PL/I programs having an average length of 853 statements has shown that the average program has 384 identifiers (variables), and these identifiers appear 1195 times within the program.[1] If such a program consisted of only a single module, the volume of variables and references to those variables would make the task of understanding the program close to impossible. Hence, one objective of partitioning the program is to reduce the number of factors that a human's mind has to keep track of simultaneously in order to comprehend the program.

Although partitioning a program is helpful for this reason, a more powerful justification for partitioning a program is that it creates a number of well-defined, documented boundaries within the program. These boundaries, or interfaces, are invaluable in the comprehension of the program. If we are interested in analyzing a particular datum, the interfaces show us where the datum is and is not used, thus narrowing our focus of attention. If we are interested in analyzing a particular piece of program code, the interfaces show us which data items are relevant and which are not, again narrowing the focus of attention. This is one reason why such entities as PL/I included-segments and COBOL performed paragraphs were excluded from the definition of the module in Chapter 2. This type of program segmentation does little to improve the structure of a program because these entities do not have explicit and identifiable interfaces.

The subject of partitioning brings the word "modularity" to mind. Because modularity is an overused and misunderstood word, the term will be avoided in this book. One good reason for avoiding the term is that a great deal of meaningless information has been written about it. It is a popular subject for trade journal articles, but close examination of the typical article will show that about 95% of the words are spent extolling the benefits of "modularity" and that little, if anything, is said about how to achieve it.

One problem with partitioning (or modularity) is that, taken by itself, it is often ineffective. Undoubtedly most programs, except for very small programs, are "modular" in some sense; yet, most programs are not well-structured. Liskov states that arbitrary partitioning can actually *increase* complexity because of two new sources: functional complexity and intermodule connection complexity.[2] She gives three examples of these sources:

1. A module performs too many related (and yet different) functions which cause its logic to be obscured.
2. Common functions are distributed throughout many modules rather than being isolated in one place.
3. Modules interact on common (global) data in unexpected ways.

Thus, while partitioning is a necessary fundamental means for reducing program complexity, it is not the only one.

HIERARCHY

The concept of hierarchical organization is of vital importance in both understanding and constructing systems. Because the average human mind has a rather small upper limit on the number of facts with which it can simultaneously deal, we find that we can better understand systems if they are hierarchically defined. For instance, we attempt to understand our own brain by studying its hierarchical organization. If we are interested in the modulation of muscle activities, we focus our attention on one of the "second-level modules" —the cerebellum. If we wish to study just voluntary movement, we can move down the hierarchy to the neocerebellum. Such hierarchical views aid our understanding by directing our span of attention and allowing us to cope with the system at various levels of detail.

For the same reasons, hierarchies aid the construction of systems. One cannot create a large program in a single leap because of the large number of factors that are simultaneously present. Hence, a hierarchical approach is an aid because it allows us to iteratively separate our ideas and to deal with increasing amounts of detail.

It should be obvious that there are many hierarchical alternatives in designing a program, not all of which are desirable. For instance, one extreme in organizing 59 modules is to make 58 modules the immediate subordinates of the top module. This "short and fat" hierarchy is usually undesirable because the top module is dealing with the integration of an excessive number of concepts and functions. Another extreme is organizing the 59 modules so that each has only a single immediate subordinate. This "tall and lean" organization is probably equally undesirable because it probably distributes the control and processing logic among the modules in an awkward way.

As was the case for partitioning, it is also true that an "in between, pleasing to the eye," hierarchy is often not an effective solution. One would hope that any particular module in the hierarchy makes few, if any, assumptions about its superordinates and that it knows nothing about its subordinates other than the interfaces to, and functions of, its immediate subordinates. However, an "eye-pleasing" hierarchy does not necessarily guarantee this. It might also be true that the hierarchy of modules does not closely reflect the hierarchy of ideas and assumptions within the program. The implication in this case is that there are implicit and obscure relationships among the modules.

Although partitioning and hierarchies are important concepts in good program design, there is a third related concept that is most important. This is maximizing the independence among the parts of the system.

INDEPENDENCE

The most important consideration in good design, and the single idea on which most of composite design is based, is the idea of *high module independence*. The objective is not simply partitioning a program into a hierarchy, but determining how to partition a program into a hierarchical structure such that each module is as independent from all other modules as possible.

Because this vital concept of independence is not widely understood, a physical analogy is helpful. Although the analogy is stronger in a larger circuit, we can examine the partitioning of the small electronic circuit in Figure 3.1. Suppose we are told that this circuit is to be partitioned into four pieces (e.g., for packaging on printed-circuit boards or into integrated circuit chips). One methodology might be to assign a unique number to each individual component in Figure 3.1. and then to pick these numbers at random, successively placing them into four groups. An alternative methodology might be drawing diagonal lines from each corner of the page, thus grouping the components into four boxes.

If we use either of these methodologies, it is likely that the end-result will exhibit two attributes:

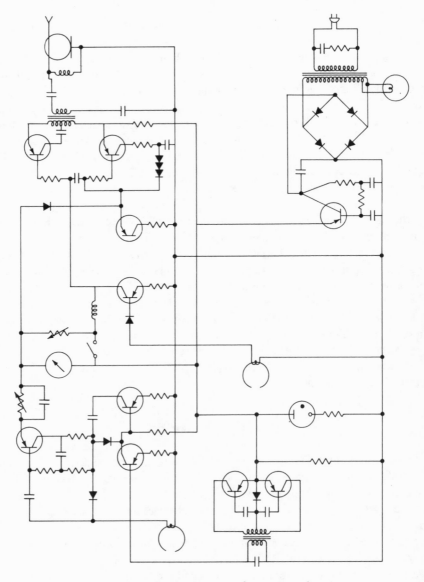

Figure 3.1   A system to be partitioned

1. There will be a large number of interconnections (wires) among the four boxes.
2. The inherent functions within the circuit (e.g., power supply, oscillator, audio amplifier) will be spread over the four boxes. Conversely, each box will perform part of a large number of functions

24

(e.g., circuit board *A* contains part of the power supply function, the transformer for the audio amplifier, and two resistors for the oscillator function).

If our product has these attributes, it will undoubtedly exhibit the following problems:

1. The system will be difficult to understand. To understand any particular aspect of the system, one will have to examine all of its parts.
2. The system will be difficult to maintain. If a design flaw is discovered in the power supply function, the change will likely ripple throughout all of the parts.
3. The system will be difficult to extend. To increase the power of the audio amplifier, one cannot simply unplug the existing amplifier and insert a more powerful one. Adding an entirely new function will be difficult because it will not be apparent how to integrate it into the existing design.
4. The probability of being able to use one of these parts in a new product will be virtually zero. The first reason is the large number of interconnections to each part. Second, our underlying motivation in reusing a part is to reuse a function, but each function is scattered among all of the parts. Third, each part performs multiple functions, some of which may be of no use in (or even interfere with) the new product.

The mistake here should be apparent. When we partitioned this system we should have organized it so that 1) the relationships among boxes were minimized and 2) the relationships among the elements of an individual box were maximized. In other words, to have achieved high independence, the system should have been partitioned so that if two components were not closely related, they would fall into separate partitions, and if two components were closely related, they would fall into the same partition.

One weakness with this analogy is that it is an after-the-fact partitioning; we already had the details (the circuit schematic) and we were looking for the best structure. Let us look at another analogy with the same weakness, but one that is more closely related to programming. We start by selecting any existing program (well-designed or poorly designed, it does not matter). The objective is to plot a point representing each statement on the graph of Figure 3.2. To do this, pick any pair of statements and analyze their relationships. If the two statements have a close data relationship (e.g., they reference the same variable), the points will be plotted close together horizontally. If the statements do not reference the same variable but do reference different fields in the same data structure, the points will be plotted "somewhat close" horizontally. If they reference completely unrelated data, the points will be separated by a large horizontal distance.

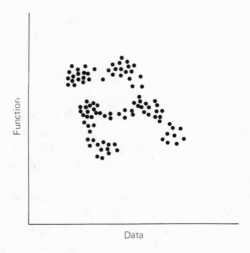

Figure 3.2   Graph of program statement relationships

Before the points are actually plotted, the functional relationship is also analyzed. If the two statements are part of the same function within the program, the points will be close vertically; if not, they are separated by a larger vertical difference.

If we obtained such a plot of the relationships among all the statements in a program, it might typically have the appearance of Figure 3.2. The important thing to notice is the *clustering effect;* there are clusters of closely related statements, and these clusters are only minimally related to one another. Now we can

Figure 3.3   The ideal module boundaries

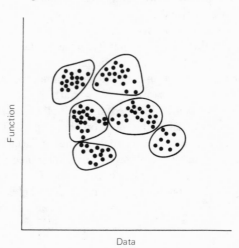

ask: Wouldn't it have been nice if the module boundaries for this program were those indicated in Figure 3.3?

Again this analogy is an after-the-fact one, and it certainly is not meant to imply that one should write the source code of a program before defining the program's structure. What it does imply, however, is that we need the foresight to define the circles or partitions properly so that when we do eventually code the program the clusters will fall within the predefined circles (the modules). The methodology of composite design is a means to this foresight.

The key to successful program structuring, therefore, is maximizing module independence. One way of viewing this is that one attempts to find the high-frequency dynamics of a system and to isolate these within single modules; simultaneously, the modules are defined such that the intermodule effects are the low-frequency dynamics. Another view of maximizing module independence is that one attempts to obstruct, as much as possible, each module's knowledge and view of the remainder of the system.

An important part of composite design is a set of measurements of module independence. The first measurement, module strength, categorizes the internal relationships of a single module. A module's strength is determined by analyzing the function(s) of the module; the design goal is to maximize this strength. The second measurement, module coupling, categorizes the direct intermodule relationships among all modules in the program. The coupling between two modules is determined by analyzing the data that are jointly referenced by the two modules and the method used to transmit the data; the design goal is to minimize the coupling among modules. Although no claim is made that module strength and coupling completely define the independence of modules (e.g., they would not point out the dependency between two modules in a gymnastics scoring program due to a joint assumption that the highest possible score is 9.95), they do define the general conditions of independence.

For a more philosophical discussion of partitioning, hierarchy, and independence in systems of any type, the works of Alexander[3] and Simon[4] are recommended.

REFERENCES

1. J. L. Elshoff, "An Analysis of Some Commercial PL/I Programs," *IEEE Transactions on Software Engineering*, SE-2(2), 1976, 113-120.
2. B. H. Liskov, "A Design Methodology for Reliable Software Systems," *Proceedings of the 1972 Fall Joint Computer Conference.* Montvale, N. J.: AFIPS Press, 1972, 191-199.
3. C. Alexander, *Notes on the Synthesis of Form.* Cambridge, Mass.: Harvard University Press, 1964.
4. H. A. Simon, *The Sciences of the Artificial.* Cambridge, Mass.: MIT Press, 1969.

EXERCISES

1. Question for thought: Project managers usually recognize the need for giving programmers an overall, global view of the program they are developing. This is not only desirable for motivational reasons (few people enjoy developing individual modules in a program if they do not understand the "big picture"), but for discovering design flaws, and for later testing and debugging. However, the goal of high module independence implies that each module should "know" as little as possible about the remainder of the system. Not only do these two goals seem contradictory, but one could argue that the former can subvert the latter because programmers could subconsciously take advantage of their global understanding when coding a module to reduce the module's independence. Think about this contradiction and how it might be dealt with in a project.

4

Module Strength

Achieving high module independence involves both the maximization of relationships within each module and the minimization of the relationships among modules. Module strength, being associated with the former, is a measurement of the relationships among the elements within a single module. Because module strength is a measurement, it can be used to evaluate the "goodness" of a particular program structure, but its main purpose is to provide an understanding of desirable and undesirable module characteristics. Therefore, module strength guides the definition of modules during the design process.

There are seven categories of module strength; the scale from highest to lowest strength is

1. Functional strength and informational strength
3. Communicational strength
4. Procedural strength
5. Classical strength
6. Logical strength
7. Coincidental strength

The two highest forms of strength are modules that perform single specific functions; the lowest form is a module that performs multiple unrelated functions. The scale indicates a relationship among the categories; for instance, a classical-strength module is more desirable than a logical-strength module. However, there is considerable overlap among the categories; for instance, an extreme case of classical strength is likely to be *less* desirable than a moderate case of logical strength. The ordering of the scale was determined by studying modules in each category and their relative effects on module reusability, error-proneness, independence, and program maintainability and extensibility.

It is important to note that the scale is not intended as a design standard; the scale does not imply that a program with a logical-strength module is a totally undesirable program. It may be true that, because of factors peculiar to the program being designed, one logical-strength module is necessary. Hopefully, however, the environment is such that the designer can objectively say "Yes, the program has a logical-strength module, and I realize the undesirable implications of such a module, but I decided to make this tradeoff for the following reasons ..." It is this type of environment that we are striving for. It is much better than the environment that creates an ad hoc design of low-strength modules because the designer neither understands the alternatives nor realizes the implications of his or her decisions.

The remainder of this chapter is an examination of each of the seven categories of strength. Because a preliminary discussion of the worst cases will help rationalize the need for the best cases, the order of presentation is from worst case to best case.

COINCIDENTAL STRENGTH

A coincidental-strength module is a module that meets either of the following criteria: 1) its function cannot be defined (i.e., the only way of describing the module is by describing its logic), or 2) it performs multiple, completely unrelated, functions.

In Chapter 3 we saw an example of the creation of coincidental-strength modules. The methodology used to partition the electronic circuit—by assigning each component a unique number, and then drawing these numbers at random and placing them in four boxes—probably created four such modules or circuit boards. Each module performed several pieces of several functions which, in some cases, would probably make it impossible to define the modules' functions.

Despite the fact that few rational people consciously attempt to create such modules, they still occasionally appear. Therefore, it is helpful to understand how they are originated. Suppose we have the task of maintaining a large monolithic FORTRAN program and, during a lull in the maintenance process, we are instructed to "modularize" the program. Knowing that "modularize" means "chop it up into pieces," we get a friend to hold up the listing of the program, and we use a machete to slice the listing into a number of pieces. Each slice of the listing becomes a module of the new "modularized" version.

If we use this partitioning method, it is likely that many of the modules will have coincidental strength. For instance, the function of one module might be "plot the x-axis of the life expectancy graph, print headings for the population graph, read the state-by-state populations for the previous 10 years, and notify the operator of the need for the occupational hazard rates." Another module in the program might contain the code of Figure 4.1. The first module has coincidental strength because it performs four functions having no apparent relationship. The second module also has coincidental strength because there is no obvious way of describing its function; the only way to define the module is by exposing its logic.

Other situations in which coincidental-strength modules arise are: 1) when

```
      SUBROUTINE A5 (MAX,A,BIG,EPSILON,ACC)
      DIMENSION A(80) ,ACC(10)
      WRITE (6, 12)
      WRITE (7, 13) MAX
   12 FORMAT ('EXTRA TRANSACTIONS IGNORED')
   13 FORMAT(F10.0)
      DO 20 I=1,80
         A(I)=0
   20 CONTINUE
    C READ CONTROL PARAMETERS
      READ(5, 14) N,EPSILON
   14 FORMAT(I2,F10.0)
      BIG=N+4*EPSILON
      DO 30 I=1,10
         ACC(I)=2*ACC(I)+SQRT(ACC(I))
   30 CONTINUE
      END
```

Figure 4.1   A coincidental-strength module

arbitrary sections of code are chopped from a program to create overlay phases (because the original program is too large for storage) and 2) when unwise programming standards, such as "every module must have less than 60 statements and more than 45 statements," are strictly followed.

One could debate whether partitioning a program into coincidental-strength modules is better than not partitioning the program at all, but one factor is readily apparent: coincidental-strength modules contribute nothing positive toward module independence. Rather than isolating the high-frequency dynamics of a system within individual modules, coincidental-strength modules do the opposite. The elements within a coincidental-strength module are only loosely, if at all, related to one another; but at the same time, they are closely related to elements within other modules.

There is some evidence, from an experiment at Indiana University, that coincidental-strength modularity is worse than none at all. [1] Given three versions of a program, one with four high-strength modules, one with no modularity (a single module), and one with "random" modularity (five modules, four of which presumably had coincidental strength), students comprehended the high-strength program best and the coincidental-strength program the least. The differences in comprehension were statistically significant.

In short, coincidental-strength modules are not independent; they tend to be closely related to their superordinate and subordinate modules. Because coincidental-strength modules perform sets of unrelated functions (and pieces of other functions) their interfaces are usually large, their probability of reuse is close to zero, and they degrade program maintainability and extensibility.

LOGICAL STRENGTH

A logical-strength module is one that performs a set of related functions, one of which is explicitly selected by the calling module. In other words, the interface to a logical-strength module includes some type of function code argument; this argument is used to dynamically select a function to be performed.

The major problem with this type of module is that it has a single interface for multiple functions. This makes the interface both more complicated than need be and more difficult to understand. This leads to serious extensibility problems. To understand this, review the interface specification in Figure 4.2.

Upon examining Figure 4.2, several problems should be apparent. The arguments have different interpretations depending on which function is invoked. Also, some of the arguments are ignored when certain of the functions are invoked. For instance, to call this module to clear the state table, one must pass four arguments; however, the last three are ignored, meaning that they are "dummies." Consider the confusion presented to the reader of the following program segment:

```
FCODE=0; /*SET FUNCTION CODE FOR CLEAR*/
CALL STATE(FCODE,DUM1,DUM2,DUM3);
/*DUM1, DUM2, AND DUM3 ARE DUMMY VARIABLES THAT ARE
  NOT USED IN THIS FUNCTION*/
```

Figure 4.2   (below) An interface to a logical-strength module

MODULE: STATE-TABLE
ARGUMENTS PASSED: 4
ARGUMENT 1: A ONE-DIGIT FUNCTION CODE
   0—CLEAR THE STATE TABLE
   1—ADD ENTRY TO STATE TABLE
   2—DELETE ENTRY FROM STATE TABLE
   3—SEARCH STATE TABLE
   4—COPY STATE TABLE TO AUDIT FILE
ARGUMENT 2: EIGHT-CHARACTER STATE NAME. THIS IS AN INPUT FOR FUNCTIONS
   1, 2, AND 3 AND IGNORED FOR 0 AND 4.
ARGUMENT 3: EIGHT-DIGIT STATE POPULATION. THIS IS AN INPUT FOR FUNCTION
   1 AND AN OUTPUT FROM FUNCTION 3.
ARGUMENT 4: ONE-DIGIT ERROR CODE. THIS IS AN OUTPUT ARGUMENT EXCEPT
   FOR FUNCTION 0, WHERE IT HAS NO MEANING. AN ERROR CODE OF 0 MEANS NO
   ERROR. FOR FUNCTION 1, 1 MEANS TABLE FULL AND 2 MEANS DUPLICATE ENTRY
   IN TABLE. FOR FUNCTIONS 2 AND 3, 1 MEANS ENTRY IS NOT PRESENT. FOR
   FUNCTION 4, 1 MEANS I/O ERROR, 2 MEANS END-OF-FILE, AND 3 MEANS EMPTY
   STATE TABLE.

If the last comment had been excluded, the program segment would be even more confusing.

Even though the interfaces to logical-strength modules tend to be obscure, there is a more significant problem—a user of one of the functions has to be cognizant of all of the functions. If one writes a module that only uses the "copy state table to audit file" function, he or she must at least be aware of the four other functions since the single interface reflects all five functions.

This problem becomes rather significant when one of the functions must be modified and the modification necessitates a change to the interface (e.g., changing the size or attributes of an argument or adding a new argument). Suppose this module is part of a large system and that two modules use the "clear" function, 10 modules use the "add" function, five other modules use the "delete" function, four use the "search" function, and one module uses the "copy" function. Suppose the "copy state table" function must be changed so that the table is copied to either the weekly audit file or the permanent audit file. Making this change requires the addition of a new argument. We then realize that rather than changing just the single module that uses this function, we must change the 21 other modules that use this interface, *even though they have nothing to do with this function* (copying a state table).

If such a change seems too expensive, we have another alternative—using one of the arguments that were unused in this function. Since argument 2 (the state name) is not used in the "copy" function, we can define a convention that a state name of AAAAAAAA indicates use of the weekly file, and BBBBBBBB indicates use of the permanent file. Needless to say, this alternative will lead to trouble. The second alternative may sound outlandish; however, compared with the task of altering 21 additional modules, we might expect the second alternative to be the most probable choice. Clearly neither alternative is desirable.

Although this example illustrates a number of problems, realize that it is only a "mild" case of logical strength. Typical logical-strength modules are worse. For instance, IBM's OS/VS2 operating system contains a logical-strength module that performs 13 functions and contains an interface of 21 pieces of data.

Notice that the logical-strength module presents us with at least one other problem: what happens when the function code is assigned a value other than its defined values? The implication is that, in addition to the defensive programming that we have already placed in the module, we also have to defend against an invalid function code and must consider the difficult question of what action to take if an invalid function code is detected.

Although logical-strength modules are undesirable, the motivation for their creation is often valid. For instance, we might have created the previous module in order to isolate all knowledge of the state table in one module. However, there is a superior way to achieve this objective without resorting to a logical-strength module; this is the informational-strength module discussed later in the chapter.

CLASSICAL STRENGTH

The next higher type of strength, but still rather low on the scale, is classical strength. A classical-strength module performs multiple sequential functions where there is a weak, but nonzero, relationship among all of the functions.

The most common type of classical-strength modules are "initialization" and "termination" modules. Such a module is one with the function "open the transaction file, open the master file, initialize the summary table, and print the report headings." A prevalent "old wives' tale" in program structuring is "every program needs an initialization module in the upper left corner and a termination module in the upper right corner."

The trouble with a classical-strength module is that its functions are only weakly related to one another and, in fact, are more closely related to functions in other modules. For instance, if one of the functions in the initialization module is "zero the summary table," it is likely that functions that reference (add to and examine) the summary table must also exist in the program and that these functions are a considerable "distance" away. Hence, a classical-strength module tends to have implicit, difficult to distinguish, relationships to other modules. Since the functions in the classical-strength module are only weakly related to one another, this type of module contributes little to the independence within the program.

The implication that initialization and termination modules have low strength often raises the question of where to perform the initialization and termination operations. The question is valid, but the answer is difficult to state at this point because it is related to the decomposition techniques in Chapters 8–12. A partial answer, however, is to "do it where it comes naturally." If a program contains a module having the function "summarize weekly transaction file in summary table," then one might expect such initialization operations as opening the transaction file and initializing the summary table to be within, or subordinate to, this module rather than collected in a separate classical-strength module.

PROCEDURAL STRENGTH

A procedural-strength module, a little higher on the strength scale, is a module that performs multiple sequential functions, where the sequential relationship among all of the functions is implied by the problem or application statement. For instance, if the problem statement (e.g., external specification) implies that when an invalid transaction is encountered, the program should skip to the next transaction file, checkpoint the master file, and display an appropriate error message, then a module having the function "skip to next transaction file, checkpoint master file, and display error message X12" has procedural strength.

Since this type of module is midway on the scale, one cannot find serious disadvantages with it, nor can one find many good things to say about it. It is above classical strength because there is a closer relationship among its elements than exists in a classical-strength module. However, the functions within a procedural-strength module are not strongly related. For instance, there is no apparent relationship between checkpointing the master file and displaying error message X12 other than the implication in the specification that, under one circumstance, they should be performed at the same time.

COMMUNICATIONAL STRENGTH

A communicational-strength module is one that performs multiple sequential functions, where the sequential relationship among all of the functions is implied by the problem or application statement, *and* where there is a data relationship among all of the functions. Hence, communicational strength is similar to procedural strength, but one additional criterion must be present—the functions must be related to one another in terms of data usage. This means, for instance, that all of the functions reference the same information; the result of the first function is the input to the second function, the result of the second is the input to the third, and so forth.

As an example, if the problem statement implies that an invalid transaction should be displayed on the terminal and written to the audit file, then a module defined as "display transaction and copy it to audit file" has communicational strength.

FUNCTIONAL STRENGTH

The highest form of strength is functional strength. One valid way of defining a functional-strength module is stating that it is anything else; that is, a module that does not have coincidental, logical, classical, procedural, or communicational strength. However, since functional strength is the goal, it should be defined in positive terms. Hence, a functional-strength module is defined as a module that performs a single specific function.

Given the comments made in defining and delineating the categories of module strength, one might get the impression that module strength is merely a matter of semantics. In other words, that by rewording a module's description (without altering the module itself), the module's strength can be altered. Of course, this impression must be false. If it was true, the strength scale would be of no use. The semantic problem arises because one can take almost any single specific function and describe it as a set of more primitive functions. For instance, "summarize transaction file" could be restated as "open transaction file, read each record and add it to summary table, and close transaction file." Even a primitive machine instruction such as ADD can be restated as "fetch operands from

35

storage and move them to processor registers A and B, set the ALU function register to add, gate A and B to the ALU, store the ALU output in storage, and set the condition code."

The question is not whether a function can also be defined as a set of more primitive functions, *but whether the opposite is true.* If a set of functions can be collectively described as a single specific function in a coherent way, then the module performing these functions has functional strength; if not, it has a lower type of strength. The module that opens the transaction file, reads records, adds them to the summary table, and closes the file can be described as performing the function "summarize transaction file"; therefore, it has functional strength. The functions "skip to the next transaction file, checkpoint master file, and display error message X12" cannot be defined accurately in a single less-primitive function; therefore, this module has procedural rather than functional strength.

Another false impression is that only the primitive modules in a program can have functional strength. This is not the case; we have already seen in Chapter 2 that the top module in a COBOL compiler is likely to have the function "compile a COBOL program." This is a single specific function and, therefore, the module has functional strength. The decomposition methods in Chapters 8–12 have the objective of producing a program structure in which every module has functional strength.

Note that the categories of strength are not mutually exclusive. This occasionally leads to confusion when categorizing a module. For instance, a functional-strength module can also meet the definition of procedural strength. When this dilemma occurs, the module is considered to have functional strength. In other words, a module has the highest type of strength whose definition it meets. However, if a module only partially meets the definition of a higher form of strength, the dilemma is not resolved this way. For instance, a module that performs five problem-related sequential functions, where three of those functions have a data relationship, is considered to have procedural, not communicational, strength.

INFORMATIONAL STRENGTH

It is often the case that a program entirely constructed with functional-strength modules still does not have a maximally independent structure. Two functional-strength modules named "build master-file record" and "validate all fields in master-file record" seem closely related. Likewise, the modules "allocate buffer from buffer pool" and "return buffer to pool" do not seem highly independent from one another. Similarly, the three functional-strength modules "insert entry in symbol table," "delete entry from symbol table," and "search symbol table" may be highly independent from the remainder of the program, but they seem closely dependent on one another. Because these three modules are dependent on the format and organization of the symbol table, it is likely that if one of the modules must be altered the other two will require corresponding changes.

The informational-strength module, a key concept in achieving maximal module independence, is a solution to these problems. One can eliminate the three symbol-table-related modules and replace them with a single informational-strength module. In fact, this is often the way informational-strength modules are used in practice. One designs the program with the objective of functional strength, then reviews the design looking for dependencies (such as those illustrated above) and removes these through the creation of informational-strength modules.

The purpose of an informational-strength module is to hide some concept, data structure, or resource within a single module. An informational-strength module has the following definition:

1. It contains multiple entry points.
2. Each entry point performs a single specific function.
3. All of the functions are related by a concept, data structure, or resource that is hidden within the module.

One can view informational-strength modules as the packaging together of related functional-strength modules. For instance, rather than creating three functional-strength modules that perform transformations on the symbol table, we can create a single informational-strength module having three entry points. Note the increase in module independence within the program. We have achieved the concept of *information hiding*[2]; that is, this informational-strength module is the only module that is sensitive to the format and organization of the symbol table. Key decisions can be made or changed concerning the symbol table (e.g., storing it sequentially, as a linked list, or as a hash table, and storing it in sorted order or not) without altering other modules.

Another "old wives' tale" in the industry is that "multiple entry-point modules are inconsistent with structured programming, since they violate the single-entry, single-exit rule." This may be valid if the code for one entry point "falls" into the code for another entry point, but the informational-strength module need not (and should not) be constructed this way. The structured programming guideline states that any block of code should have only a single point of entry and a single point of exit. Consistency with the spirit of structured programming is achieved by adding the additional criterion:

4. There are no control-flow connections among the logic for each function.

In other words, an informational-strength module fits the model in Figure 4.3 (illustrated in PL/I).

One alternative that comes to mind to achieve the same effect is constructing the module with a single entry point and passing a function-code argument specifying the function to be performed. However, this is the logical-strength module discussed earlier, and this alternative is undesirable. The alternative to

```
function1: PROCEDURE(parameters);
data declarations for hidden concept

    local data declarations for function1
    code for function1
RETURN;
function2: ENTRY(parameters);
  local data declarations for function2
    code for function2
RETURN;
function3: ENTRY(parameters);
    local data declarations for function3
    code for function3
RETURN;
END;
```

Figure 4.3   Model of a three-function informational-strength module

Figure 4.4   Informational-strength version of the state-table module

```
MODULE: STATE-TABLE
ENTRY: CLEAR-STATE-TABLE
  NO ARGUMENTS
ENTRY: ADD-ENTRY-TO-STATE-TABLE
  ARG1: EIGHT-CHARACTER STATE NAME (INPUT)
  ARG2: EIGHT-DIGIT STATE POPULATION (INPUT)
  ARG3: ONE-DIGIT ERROR CODE (OUTPUT)
    0=NO ERROR, 1=TABLE FULL, 2=DUPLICATE ENTRY IN TABLE
ENTRY: DELETE-ENTRY-FROM-STATE-TABLE
  ARG1: EIGHT-CHARACTER STATE NAME (INPUT)
  ARG2: ONE-DIGIT ERROR CODE (OUTPUT)
    0=NO ERROR, 1=ENTRY NOT IN TABLE
ENTRY: SEARCH-STATE-TABLE
  ARG1: EIGHT-CHARACTER STATE NAME (INPUT)
  ARG2: EIGHT-DIGIT STATE POPULATION (OUTPUT)
  ARG3: ONE-DIGIT ERROR CODE (OUTPUT)
    0=NO ERROR, 1=ENTRY NOT IN TABLE
ENTRY: COPY-STATE-TABLE-TO-AUDIT-FILE
  ARG1: ONE-DIGIT ERROR CODE (OUTPUT)
    0=NO ERROR, 1=I/O ERROR, 2=END-OF-FILE,
    3=EMPTY STATE TABLE
```

the earlier logical-strength example should now be obvious. The "state-table" module would contain five entry points, one for each function. The function-code argument is no longer needed, each interface is simpler, the arguments no longer have different interpretations for different functions, and modules using one of these interfaces need not know of the other interfaces. The new interface specification is shown in Figure 4.4. The program modification (adding another argument for the "copy" function) that caused so much anguish with the logical-strength alternative (because we had to modify 23 modules) now only requires the alteration of two modules.

In summary, one key design goal in structuring a program is to create only functional-strength and informational-strength modules. Such modules optimize the module independence of the program, decrease the program's susceptibility to errors, enhance the program's extensibility, and have a higher-than-normal probability of being reused in multiple contexts in this program and in future programs.

REFERENCES

1. B. Shneiderman and R. Mayer, "Towards a Cognitive Model of Programmer Behavior," TR-37, Indiana University, Bloomington, Ind., 1975.
2. D. L. Parnas, "On the Criteria to be Used in Decomposing Systems into Modules," *Communications of the ACM,* 15(12), 1972, 1053–1058.

EXERCISES

1. Since logical-strength modules are quite common and yet quite undesirable, find one in an existing program and study it with respect to the disadvantages attributed to logical-strength modules.

2. Take an existing program and categorize the strength of its modules. Next, see if you can confirm the relationships between each module's strength and its effect on independence, complexity, error-proneness, reusability, extensibility, and maintainability.

3. The following are brief functional descriptions of modules. Although the descriptions are terse and these modules are taken out of context, study each description and determine the probable strength of each module.
   a. Print and punch the output file
   b. Update, add, or delete a record on the master file
   c. Sort the file of detail records
   d. Read the next transaction, edit it, and display it to the tape operator
   e. Write a message to operator (input is a message code number)
   f. Allocate or free the storage subpool
   g. Read or write an inventory record (two entry points)
   h. Obtain the next L05 record

i. Initialize the work areas needed to generate the object code
j. Calculate new trajectory and send it to terminal
k. Update record in data base and read next transaction
l. Print the next line, find substring in second parameter, and convert third parameter from character to floating-point
m. Allocate a storage area (input describes the amount to be allocated)
n. Read the next transaction or increment print-line count or initialize summary table (one of the arguments is a function code)
o. Find best potential date for this person (if there is none with consistent desires, return "no date found" indicator.)
p. Add a node to the tree, delete a node from the tree, search the tree for a node, or produce the postorder view of the tree (four entry points)
q. Initialize region table, close country file, open next transaction file, and print summary line
r. Display shut-down message on all terminals
s. Format screen for part display and read part record from data base
t. Mainline control module
u. Obtain first transaction, obtain lowest and highest keys in master file, and print page headings
v. Search region table, search salary table, or save employee list on spill file (three entry points)

5

Module Coupling

In Chapter 4 maximization of relationships within each module was considered as a means for achieving high module independence. Module strength was the main concern in maximizing such relationships *within* a module; but, as was seen, it did have some effect on intermodule relationships.

The subject of module coupling is entirely concerned with intermodule relationships. Minimizing module coupling is a process of both eliminating unnecessary relationships among modules and minimizing the tightness of those relationships that are necessary.

The order of discussion (strength, then coupling) does not imply that module coupling is of lesser importance; module strength and coupling are considered to be equally important. Module strength was discussed first because it is a more difficult concept. As evidence of this, it is impossible to write a "strength-analysis program"—a program that examines another program and categorizes the strengths of its modules. However, this is not the case for module coupling; excepting one problem area, one could write a program that examines another program and categorizes the couplings among its modules.

As was the case for module strength, module coupling is a measurement, and it can be used to evaluate the "goodness" of a program structure. However, its major purpose is to provide an understanding of desirable and undesirable module relationships, thus guiding the program designer in the establishment of module interfaces. There are seven categories of module coupling; the scale from lowest coupling (best case) to tightest coupling (worst case) is

1. No direct coupling
2. Data coupling
3. Stamp coupling
4. Control coupling
5. External coupling
6. Common coupling
7. Content coupling

Since module coupling describes intermodule relationships, it is only used when speaking of more than one module. That is, the statement that module A is data coupled has no meaning, but the statement that modules A and B are data coupled does have meaning.

The lowest form of coupling (no coupling) is not used as a design guideline, although it is used when analyzing relationships in an existing design. Its definition is "none of the below," that is, two modules exhibit no direct coupling if they are not data, stamp, control, external, common, or content coupled. Data coupling is the next lowest form of coupling, and it serves as the primary design goal. Data coupling occurs when all communication between two modules is in the form of arguments/parameters and each argument is homogeneous (i.e., not a heterogeneous aggregate of data such as a PL/I or COBOL structure).

As was the case with the strength scale, the coupling scale implies an order of desirability among the types of coupling, but the categories do overlap. For instance, an extreme case of stamp coupling is *less* desirable than a mild case of control coupling. The scale was ordered by studying modules in each category and their relative effects on module reusability, error-proneness, difficulty of testing and debugging, independence, maintainability, and extensibility. As was advised with module strength, be cautious about interpreting the scale as a set of standards. The intent of the scale is to introduce more analysis and objectivity into the design process. The designer may still rationalize an occasional need for a tighter (less desirable) form of coupling, but, in doing so, he or she should be able to explain why the negative implications are outweighed by some other factor.

CONTENT COUPLING

Two modules are content coupled if one *directly* references the insides of the other or if the normal linkage conventions between the modules are bypassed (e.g., a module branches to, rather than calls, the other module). The word "directly" describes a relationship that is not resolved by some other binding program or mechanism, such as a linkage editor.

As an example, two assembly-language modules A and B are content coupled if A references a word at some numerical displacement within B. It is not difficult to see that A and B are extremely dependent. Almost any change to module B, or even just recompiling B with a different version of the compiler (or assembler), will require a change to module A.

Fortunately there are several factors mitigating the practice of content coupling. First, virtually everyone recognizes it as a poor programming practice. Secondly, content coupling is extremely difficult to create in a high-level language program. (But it is not impossible; for instance, holes in most implementations of PL/I allow a devious programmer to create content-coupled PL/I modules.)

Despite these factors, content coupling does occur occasionally. For example, Spier describes a disastrous sequence of events, initiated by an occurrence of content coupling, in the evolution of a compiler.[1] In an early version of the compiler, a module named FLUSH performed several operations and then called a module named SWITCH before returning. This situation was spotted by a programmer. In an attempt to "optimize" the program, the programmer changed the call to an absolute branch to SWITCH, thus content coupling the two modules. This change was found to work correctly, for the RETURN statement in SWITCH returned control to the point of the last call. When SWITCH was called directly, control returned to its calling module; when SWITCH was branched to from FLUSH, control returned to the caller of FLUSH.

Because this change removed some linkage overhead, similar changes were made in the compiler. As a result, the compiler ended up with a curious mixture of call/returns and absolute branches among modules. The compiler seemed to function properly because the "optimizing wizard" saw to the unstated convention that each logical path contain an equal number of CALLs and RETURNs.

Time passed and future modifications to the compiler resulted in new instances in which SWITCH was to be invoked independently of FLUSH. Reading the code and seeing that the apparent convention was to branch to SWITCH rather than call it, the new programmers adopted the convention. However, since SWITCH returned to the last address on the call/return stack, the compiler began to fail unpredictably because there was not always a valid return address on the stack. Recognizing that the failure was due to an unequal number of CALLs and RETURNs, but making the mistake of correcting the symptom rather than the problem, code was added to place dummy return addresses in the stack between compilation passes. However, this change was not completely successful; it caused the stack to have a surplus of return addresses under certain conditions thus leading to stack-overflow errors. Once again, the new symptom rather than the problem was rectified. The size of the stack was increased, but this just made the errors more unpredictable. At this point Spier was called in to lend a hand. He reconstructed the sequence of events and recommended that the entire compiler be written off as a loss.

COMMON COUPLING

Common coupling, next to worst on the scale, occurs among a group of modules that reference a global data structure. Common coupling is named after the FORTRAN COMMON statement, a statement that defines a globally accessible collection of data. If a set of PL/I modules contains the following statement, the modules are common coupled with one another.

```
DECLARE 1  GBLAREA EXTERNAL, /*GLOBAL WORK AREA*/
           2 NUMLINES FIXED DECIMAL (3),
           2 LISTHEAD POINTER,
```

2 YTD__AMT FIXED DECIMAL (7,2),

2 REGION CHARACTER (4),

2 THISYEAR FIXED DECIMAL (4);

Given that common coupling is next to worst on the scale and that its use is widespread, a detailed analysis of its problems is worthwhile. Eight serious problems associated with common coupling are defined below.

1. The use of global data appears to contradict the spirit of structured programming because global data inhibits program readability. Consider the following program segment:

   DO WHILE (RECORDS=0);
      CALL GET1(X,Y);
      IF (Y=0) THEN CALL INPLACE(X,Y);
              ELSE CALL FINDIMM(Z);
   END;

   If we are attempting to understand this set of statements (e.g., to make a change or find a bug), the first question that comes to mind is: under what conditions does the loop terminate? If RECORDS is not global and certain other definable programming practices are not used (e.g., aliasing or overlaying variables), the answer is none. However, if RECORDS is global, the answer is difficult. We have no idea which of the modules GET1, INPLACE, and FINDIMM references RECORDS, so we must examine these three modules. Furthermore, because RECORDS is global, it could be referenced *anywhere*. Therefore, in addition to examining GET1, INPLACE, and FINDIMM, we must examine all modules that are subordinate to these three modules. Even worse, if this code is part of a system containing asynchronously executing processes or tasks, examination of all of the subordinate modules is insufficient; every module in each of the other processes could potentially reference RECORDS. Thus, the top-to-bottom readability quality that structured code is supposed to have is destroyed by the use of global data.

2. Global data reduces program intelligibility in a second way: by giving modules *side-effects*. For instance, if we encounter the statement

   CALL GETNEXTTRANS (TRANSACTION, ERRCODE)

   we may decide that we understand what this module does. However, if GETNEXTTRANS references a global variable (e.g., it increments a global transaction counter), this module has a side-effect—a form of data communication that is not apparent in the interface. Such side-effects impede the process of understanding the program.

3. Similar to the effect of logical-strength modules, global data struc-

tures also introduce dependencies among apparently unrelated modules. Assume that the previous PL/I global structure GBL-AREA is used in a program, that modules A and B reference only YTD_AMT, and modules C and D reference only REGION. The definition for common coupling states that A, B, C, and D are common coupled to one another. One reason is that a modification to modules A and B that requires an expansion of the size of YTD_AMT will unexpectedly require a change to C and D (or, at the minimum, a recompilation) because the location of REGION in the shared data structure has changed.

4. Modules that reference global data are difficult to use in multiple contexts in the program. Consider two modules: the first receives its inputs as dynamic parameters and the second receives one or more inputs from a global area. The latter module is likely to be more difficult to use in other contexts because it always obtains its input from one fixed location. If it has multiple calling modules, these modules must place the input in this fixed location. However, because each module cannot be sure that some other module is using this area, each calling module might have to save and restore the data in the global area. This results in additional complexity. Furthermore, if there is any parallel processing or multitasking in the program, such mechanisms as semaphores, gates, or enqueue/dequeues must be added to the program to serialize use of the global area.

5. Likewise, modules that reference global data are difficult to use in other (i.e., future) programs. The reason is that common-coupled modules are bound together through variable names. If a module only communicates through parameters, its calling modules need not know the names of these parameters (i.e., argument and parameter names can differ). But if a module uses global data, related modules must refer to this data with the same name. This extra naming dependency makes common-coupled modules more difficult to reuse.

6. Module reusability is complicated further if the global data is a structure. If it is, one might have to artificially create this structure in a future program in order to use a common-coupled module. Consider the earlier PL/I global structure and module B which uses only the field YTD_AMT. To use module B in a new program, one has to construct the global data structure. It is probably true that this structure has no meaning in the new program, but it must be defined so that B can refer to its field YTD_AMT. This means the the structure is "faked" in the new program; the only field that has meaning is YTD_AMT. Obviously this leads to additional work and obscurity.

7. Another serious problem associated with common coupling is that the use of global data structures exposes a module to more data than necessary. Consider a module that refers to YTD—AMT in the global structure. Because YTD—AMT is in the structure, the module must contain a definition of the entire structure. Hence, there are variables in the module's listing that are not referenced, a possible source of confusion. A larger problem is that the module has *addressability* to this unneeded data. The module might inadvertently alter this data, leading to an obscure error. A more frequent problem is that the programmer might attempt to take advantage of the presence of this additional data, thus reducing further the independence within the program.

8. Probably the most significant problem with global data is that it defeats attempts to manage and control the *data access* within a program. In the implementation of a large program or system, one vital factor to be controlled is data access. This means one must understand to which data each module has access and control the usage of data within the program. If the program contains no global data, then no single programmer can make a unilateral decision to reference a new datum; at the least, the cooperation of other programmers must be solicited in order to obtain new parameters. However, if global data is present, an individual programmer can usually reference it unilaterally by simply adding the appropriate statement to his module and thus gain access to a piece of data without anyone else knowing about it. This point is not intended to imply that programmers are devious. However, programmers are notorious for taking shortsighted shortcuts when under pressure (e.g., when attempting to correct an error).

These last two points were particularly severe sources of difficulty in the development and maintenance of IBM's OS/360 operating system and its offspring (OS/VS1 and OS/VS2). Much of the data in the system is global, and most of the thousands of modules in the system reference this data, leading to excessive complexity and serious extensibility and debugging problems. For example, the system's "task control blocks," theoretically a set of private control tables intended for use by only a few task-dispatching modules, are referenced by literally thousands of modules.

In spite of this list of serious consequences of global data, people still defend its use by using one of two arguments: *my* program cannot be designed without global data, or eliminating global data leads to performance problems because of excessive argument transmission. The first argument is patently false and the second argument usually comes from the misinformed.

Despite the warning in Chapter 1 about the lack of "mathematical theorems of composite design," a few theorems can be developed; one of these concerns global data. The theorem states that global data is unnecessary because any program with global data can be transformed into an equivalent program with no global data. The proof is quite trivial. Find a global variable or structure and make it nonglobal by creating a new module and hiding the data as local data within this module. Find all previous operations (e.g., references and alterations) on this global data and make these the functions of the new module (i.e., make it an informational-strength module). Finally, remove these operations from the other modules and replace the operations with calls to the new module.

Although this proves that global data can always be eliminated, a warning is in order: the proof is just a proof, not a design method. One does not design a program by first designing it with global data and then by using this process to remove the global data. This warning is given because an analogous situation exists with structured programming. An early structured programming "theorem" showed that a program with GO TO statements could be transformed into an equivalent program without GO TOs. Unfortunately, a few early disciples interpreted this proof as a methodology to create structured programs, and their resultant programs were usually found to be "unstructured programs without GO TO statements."

The second argument, the performance problem, is not a significant one. If we are using a language with automatic storage allocation (e.g., PL/I, APL), the transmission of arguments is just a miniscule part of the cost of a CALL statement. Therefore, it should not be a concern. If the language has no automatic storage allocation (e.g., COBOL, FORTRAN), the execution time of a CALL statement is less; therefore, the relative cost of argument transmission is higher. In either case the cost can be measured in microseconds. However, since this performance question is often posed, let us assume that the people asking the question have programs with efficiency troubles. It seems rather unlikely that shaving microseconds from CALL statements will eliminate these troubles; more fruitful concerns are looking for better algorithms, improving the usage of resources, reducing page faults, and so on. If the response to these ideas is that the program has already been optimized in these areas, and it is running on the fastest hardware available, then the program is helplessly in trouble. Saving a few microseconds by using global data may help a little today, but when the usage of the program increases by a few percent tomorrow or when someone adds just one more terminal, the program will be worse. Not only will the efficiency problems be back, but all the problems associated with global data will also return.

EXTERNAL COUPLING

Slightly higher on the coupling scale is external coupling. A group of modules are external coupled if they are not content or common coupled and if they reference a homogeneous global data item. For instance, if a set of PL/I modules contains the statement

DECLARE YTD__AMT FIXED DECIMAL (7,2) EXTERNAL;

then they are external coupled with one another. External coupling in FOR-TRAN is associated with the use of labeled-common areas with one variable per label; common coupling is associated with the use of a blank-common area.

External coupling is similar to common coupling in that global data is involved. However, common coupling is associated with global data that is heterogeneous in format or meaning, while external coupling is associated with homogeneous global data. For purposes here, "homogeneous data" is defined as

1. A single scalar variable (e.g., number, character string)
2. A list or table where each entry has only one field
3. An array, providing that each element has the same meaning. (One could define an array where elements have different meanings; for example, the first element is gross pay, the second is the federal tax withholding, the third the FICA deduction, and so on. However, this will be considered a heterogeneous data collection.)

External coupling exhibits some, but not all, of the problems associated with common coupling. Problems 1 (readability), 2 (side-effects), 4 (use in multiple contexts), 5 (naming dependencies), and 8 (uncontrolled data access) are still present. Problems 3 (extra module interdependencies), 6 (creating dummy structures), and 7 (exposure to unnecessary data) disappear because the global data is not a heterogeneous structure. Hence, external coupling is an improvement over common coupling, but it is still undesirable.

CONTROL COUPLING

Control coupling is related to the kind of information transmitted between modules. Two modules are control coupled if they are not content, common, or external coupled and if one module explicitly controls the logic of the other, that is, one module passes an explicit element of control to the other module. Examples of "elements of control" are function codes transmitted to logical-strength modules, control-switch arguments, and module-name arguments.

Control coupling usually implies that one module knows something about the logic of the other module; thus, the two modules are not highly independent. If module A passes a control switch to module B, and to module A the control switch means "if on, perform this extra test," then A is aware of part of the logic of module B. If module A passes a module-name argument (e.g., in PL/I, an entry variable) to module B, then A knows something about the insides of module B: A knows that B calls other modules.

Since most modules perform some type of test or decision on their arguments or parameters, the question of what is an "element of control" and what is not arises. The question is resolved by studying how the sending module perceives the data. If the sending module perceives an argument as controlling the function or logic of the receiving module, then the argument is an element of control and the modules are control coupled. If the sending module does not perceive the interface data as controlling the function or logic of the other module, then the modules are not control coupled regardless of how the data are used by the receiving module.

The sending and receiving modules need not signify, respectively, the calling and called modules; in fact, the situation may be reversed. Such a situation of control coupling is even less desirable. In Figure 5.1 one of the outputs on interface 2 is an error code. The error code convention is that if the error code is returned with the value 101, the broker invoice is invalid and module "apply invoices" is supposed to prompt the terminal user for a correction. If the error code is 102, the broker invoice is hopelessly wrong and module "apply invoices" is directed to give up and proceed to the next invoice. Hence, modules "apply invoices" and "update data base" are control coupled because the latter is explicitly directing the logic of, and contains assumptions about, the former. This type of subordinate-to-superordinate control coupling is particularly undesirable because it represents an *inversion of control.* A subordinate module is directing the operations of its superordinates, thus violating one of the basic properties of hierarchies as discussed in Chapter 3.

Control coupling also arises in other forms, for example, the use of inter-module on-units in a language such as PL/I. Assume that, in Figure 5.2, module A contains an on-unit for a condition such as end of file or division by zero, and this on-unit is enabled during the times that A calls its subordinates. This means that an occurrence of the condition in module D will cause D's execution to be suspended and control given to the on-unit in module A. This usually implies that module A either knows something about the logic of its subordinate modules or that the subordinate modules know of the presence of the on-unit in module A. Hence, if a module contains an on-unit that is enabled during the execution of subordinate modules, we will consider that module to be control coupled to each subordinate module in which that condition can potentially arise.

Figure 5.1   An occurrence of control coupling

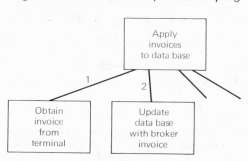

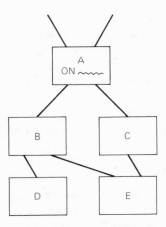

Figure 5.2   Control coupling resulting from an on-unit

STAMP COUPLING

Two modules are stamp coupled if they are not content, common, external, or control coupled and if they reference the same nonglobal data structure. Stamp coupling is similar to common coupling; the exception is that with stamp coupling the data structure is not global (e.g., it is passed among modules as an argument).

As an example, consider an employee personnel system that contains a module with the function "verify reasonableness of employee salary." Given an employee's annual salary, job level, and current performance-appraisal rating, the module indicates whether the employee is being paid within reasonable bounds or whether he or she is significantly over- or under-paid.

Assume that this system contains a data base of employee personnel records and the three pieces of information described above are three of the 47 fields in the record. If the input to the module is the personnel record, then this module is stamp coupled to all other modules that are sensitive to the format of the record. For instance, the module might be invoked by the statement

CALL VERSAL (EMPRECORD,REASONABLE__CODE)

and the module contains a definition of the employee record structure (possibly a compile-time included or copied definition) from which it extracts the three pieces of data.

Although stamp coupling has none of the problems directly associated with global data, its problems are similar to a few of those inherent in common coupling. Since module VERSAL is dependent upon the format of the personnel record, an unrelated change in the record will require a change to VERSAL (or

50

at least a recompilation). If the record contains an education-code field and this field must be expanded, not only do the modules that refer to this field have to be changed, but all other modules (including VERSAL) that are stamp coupled via the record have to be changed. Thus stamp coupling introduces dependencies among apparently unrelated modules.

Stamp-coupled modules are also somewhat difficult to reuse in other programs. Suppose that a subsidiary to this company has identical salary guidelines but a totally different personnel record. VERSAL might be useful in the subsidiary's programs, but it cannot be used unless a properly formatted personnel record is "faked" and passed to VERSAL.

Stamp coupling also exposes a module to more data than is necessary. Although VERSAL only references three fields, it has access to the other 44 fields. This increases the complexity of the module, increases the consequences of an error, and tempts the programmer to make use of the extra information. Hence, in comparing stamp coupling to the eight problems of common coupling, stamp coupling does not exhibit problems 1, 2, 4, and 5; it lessens, but does not eliminate, problem 8; and it retains problems 3, 6, and 7.

Notice that stamp coupling is present among a set of modules that are sensitive to the format of a nonglobal data structure, regardless of how the structure is transmitted from one module to another. If VERSAL receives the personnel record as a parameter, it is stamp coupled to all modules that refer to the fields within the record. Passing the *address* of the record to VERSAL does not eliminate its stamp coupling. For instance, if the first few statements of VERSAL are

```
VERSAL: PROCEDURE (ERPTR,RCODE);
    DECLARE ERPTR POINTER;
    DECLARE 1 EMPRECORD BASED (ERPTR),
        2 EMPNAME CHARACTER (12),
```

then VERSAL is still stamp coupled. If a module obtains the record by reading it from the data base, it is still stamp coupled to all other modules that contain a definition of the record.

DATA COUPLING

A solution to the problems of the VERSAL module is to recognize that VERSAL need not be aware of the personnel record at all. Since it needs three pieces of input data and returns one output, its first statement can be defined as

```
VERSAL: PROCEDURE(ANNSALARY,JOBLEVEL,
            PRATING,REASONABLE__CODE);
```

and VERSAL is defined to be data coupled to its immediate superordinate modules.

Two modules are defined as being data coupled 1) if they are not content, common, external, control, or stamp coupled, 2) if the modules directly communicate with one another (e.g., one module calls the other module), and 3) if all interface data (e.g., input and output arguments) between the modules are homogeneous data items. (As before, a "homogeneous data item" is a scalar, a single-field-per-entry table or list, or an array where each element has the same meaning.)

The advantages of the data-coupled version of VERSAL should be obvious. Since VERSAL is no longer dependent on the personnel record, changes to the record are much less likely to affect VERSAL. Also, VERSAL has an increased chance of being usable in other programs, and VERSAL is not exposed to extraneous data. Furthermore, the scope of coupling is reduced since VERSAL is now considered as being data coupled to only its calling modules. Hence, data coupling is found to have a beneficial effect on module independence, module reusability, error-proneness, extensibility, maintainability, and ease of testing.

People occasionally react negatively to the idea of data coupling because of the belief that it will lead to excessively long argument/parameter lists. First, the belief is usually wrong; if the program has been decomposed correctly, the average number of arguments passed between modules will typically be less than six or seven. Second, and in addition to the other advantages of data coupling, the argument/parameter list should be viewed as an excellent substitute for the documentation (e.g., comment statements) that would otherwise be necessary to explain what data elements are used by the module. Finally, in most compilers, the performance difference between passing one or ten arguments is either zero or negligible.

MINIMIZING STAMP COUPLING

Since the use of stamp coupling is widespread today, particularly because of increased interest in data base applications, it is worthwhile to look at three ways of minimizing the number of occurrences of stamp-coupled modules.

The first way to limit stamp coupling is to replace it with data coupling where possible. Many instances of stamp coupling are similar to the VERSAL module discussed earlier. If a module needs access to only a few fields in a structure, it is more desirable to pass the needed fields as arguments, rather than passing the structure.

A second method for avoiding stamp coupling is to use informational-strength modules. The informational-strength module is an ideal way to eliminate stamp coupling. If all of the transformations on a structure (e.g., a particular data base record) can be isolated to a single informational-strength module, then all stamp coupling via this structure is eliminated.

A final way to reduce stamp coupling is to pass structures indirectly. This is so that modules that must receive a structure and pass it on to a subordinate are not unnecessarily stamp coupled through the structure. Consider the program

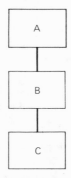

Figure 5.3   Eliminating stamp coupling from module B

structure in Figure 5.3. Assume that an input to B is a structure S, but that B has no need to know the organization of structure S; B passes S to C, which is sensitive to the structure of S. The problem is that B must contain a declaration for the structure S, even though B only passes S to C and has no need to reference the contents of S. Thus, B is unnecessarily stamp coupled to A and C. Situations like this occur in many programs where a record or structure is passed from module to module, but only a subset of the modules actually need to know the format of the structure.

A solution is to pass structure S indirectly, for instance, as a PL/I pointer variable. The input parameter to B is a pointer variable and B passes this to C. B only declares the parameter as a pointer and does not know the organization of S. Module C contains a declaration for S which is based on the pointer parameter. This removes the stamp coupling from module B. Note that this is also often needed when using reentrant informational-strength modules; that is, the definition of a structure is hidden within the informational-strength module, but the address of the structure must be dynamically carried from module to module if the program is to be reentrant.

The drawback to this solution is that PL/I pointer variables are used and, because of their generality, they are prone to errors. A data type called a *name*, which satisfies this need yet is more restrictive than the pointer data type, has been proposed.[2]

COUPLING TRADEOFFS

As was mentioned at the beginning of the chapter, the coupling scale is not intended as an absolute standard; tradeoffs in favor of a tighter form of coupling are occasionally warranted. A few typical tradeoffs are discussed below.

A question that often arises in programs that issue a large number of error messages is how to package the error messages. The two main alternatives are

1. Place the text of each message in the modules that detect the error conditions. Each module will write the message directly or possibly call a "write message" module to which the input is the message text.
2. Place the texts of all messages in a single module. Each module that detects an error will call this common module and pass it a number or the code of the message to be written.

The second alternative is a case of control coupling. All modules that call the message module are control coupled to it because of the mutual assumption of a message-number to message-text convention. However, this alternative is often the desirable one. With this alternative, the working-set size of programs in a virtual storage environment is reduced (because the messages take up no real-storage space unless a message is in the process of being written), mass revision or translation of the messages is easier, the messages usually end up worded with more consistency, and redundant copies of messages are eliminated. A further advantage is that a future decision to store the message texts on an external medium (e.g., an indexed file) is more easily implemented.

A second frequent tradeoff is that of stamp versus data coupling. In the case of the VERSAL example discussed earlier, data coupling seemed more desirable, but this alternative has one drawback. The ANNSALARY, JOBLEVEL, and PRATING parameter definitions are "hardcoded" into VERSAL. If the attributes of the corresponding fields in the personnel record change, then VERSAL must be altered, not just recompiled with a new compile-time copy of the personnel record. However, this drawback is often a figment of the imagination. If the module contains local temporary variables, then the module probably must be changed anyway to alter the attributes of these variables, rather than simply be recompiled. Moreover, the advantages of data coupling usually outweigh this possible drawback, but this still raises several questions. When is it more desirable to pass the structure as an argument instead of the individual fields? Would we select the data-coupling alternative if VERSAL needed 42 of the 47 fields?

There are no fixed answers to these questions, but the fact that the questions even arise is important because they are signs that we are *thinking* or studying alternatives. This in itself is an important achievement. Perhaps at the risk of overgeneralizing, if a module must reference a majority of the fields in a structure or if the module's function is directly associated with the structure (e.g., "validate fields in a personnel record," "display formatted part record on screen"), then passing the structure as a whole is probably more desirable. Otherwise, the data coupling alternative seems more desirable.

REFERENCES

1. M. J. Spier, "Software Malpractice—A Distasteful Experience," *Software—Practice and Experience*, 6 (3), 1976, 293–299.
2. G. J. Myers, "Composite Design Facilities of Six Programming Languages," *IBM Systems Journal*, 15(3), 1976, 212–224.

EXERCISES

1. The introduction to the chapter stated that, except for one problem area, a coupling-analysis program could be written. What is this problem area? That is, what type of coupling can only be determined by human interpretation?

2. Determine the coupling between all pairs (21 combinations) of modules in the diagram below. In addition to the interfaces described below, modules A, F, and G reference global data structure XYZ and modules A and C reference a global array ITAB.

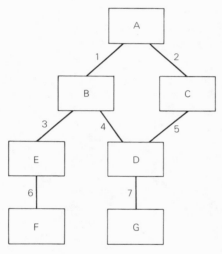

	IN	OUT
1	1 data item	1 data item
2	1 data item	1 data item
3	data base record and function code	nothing
4	nothing	list of employee names
5	nothing	list of employee names
6	data base record	nothing
7	man number	employee name

3. Which module in the above program appears to have the closest relationship to (least independence from) the remainder of the program?

4. The answers to exercise 2 showed that there was no direct coupling between some of the modules. However, is it possible to argue that there is some type of coupling (e.g., indirect coupling) among all modules in a program?

5. Take an existing program and categorize the coupling among all pairs of modules. Next, see if you can confirm the relationships between coupling and its effect on independence, complexity, error-proneness, reusability, extensibility, maintainability, and ease of testing.

6

Other Design Objectives

Although maximizing module strength and minimizing module coupling are key considerations in achieving an optimal program structure, they are not the only considerations. This chapter discusses a set of secondary design guidelines or heuristics which contribute to a well-designed program structure.

MODULE SIZE

If one adopted maximum module strength and minimum module coupling as the only design considerations, the best program structure would appear to be the single-module, monolithic program. If the program performs a single function, then this module has functional strength and module coupling is completely minimized since there are no other modules to which this module is coupled.

Clearly there is something wrong with this approach. The missing ingredient is the consideration of partitioning as discussed in Chapter 3. Partitioning has the effects of 1) reducing to a manageable number the statements or variables that must be simultaneously understood and 2) introducing a set of well-defined boundaries into the program. The average size of the modules is a reasonable measure of the degree of partitioning within a program.

Experience has shown that a well-structured program has an average module size of 40 to 50 high-level-language executable statements (i.e., excluding declarative and comment statements), with the large majority of the modules falling in the range of 10 to 100 statements. There will be occasions where modules will have fewer than 10 statements or more than 100, but these occasions should be minimized and carefully justified. If a program contains too many small modules, a person attempting to understand the program will have too small of an attention span. He or she will have to jump frequently from module to module, thus interrupting too often the train of thought. Conversely, a program with too many large modules has the problems associated with insufficient partitioning: too few well-defined interfaces and too many simultaneous thoughts.

Experience also indicates that the optimal average module size varies slightly with the overall size of the program. As a very general guideline, the average module size in a well-structured small program (a few hundred executable statements) is about 30 statements. For a "medium size" program (a few thousand statements), an average of 40–50 statements is a good guideline. For large programs (over 10,000 statements), the optimal average module size is probably between 100 and 150 statements.* Please note that all of these numbers are guidelines and averages. Adopting them as absolute standards, and thus forcing the break-up or combination of modules that fall outside of the standards, can lead to the creation of low-strength modules.

One exception to these guidelines is the informational-strength module. A corresponding guideline for informational-strength modules is that they should contain, on the average, 40–50 statements or less per entry point.

OTHER FACTORS OF MODULE INDEPENDENCE

Although module strength and coupling are important measurements of module independence, there are additional factors that influence module independence. It is difficult to generalize these other factors because they seem to be peculiar to the particular program being designed. However, it is important to identify them and then to use them to increase even further the independence among modules.

As an example, consider a program whose inputs are terminal commands. The general form of the terminal command is

cmd-name keyword(operand,operand, . . .) keyword (. . .) . . .

Key factors in this program related to module independence are

1. Knowledge of the overall syntactic structure of the commands
2. Knowledge of the command names
3. Knowledge of the keywords and operands (e.g., spelling and semantics) of each command type

These factors can be used to establish the following design objectives for this program:

1. Only one module should be sensitive to the overall syntactic structure of the commands so that a change to this structure (e.g., changing the parentheses to brackets) requires changing only one module.

---

*These guidelines seem to imply that the optimal average module size is approximately equal to the square root of the number of executable statements in the program, but the existence of such a "fundamental law" is not claimed.

2. Only one module should know the command names so that adding a new command requires changing only one existing module.
3. Only one module (or a small number) should be sensitive to the keywords and operands of each particular command type.

Other factors often present are associated with input/output operations. If a program uses several files, it is desirable to consolidate operations on each file to individual modules (e.g., informational-strength modules) so that only a single module is sensitive to the characteristics of each file. As another example, in an automobile-insurance system it may be desirable to isolate, within individual modules, all factors peculiar to each state's automobile-insurance legislation.

INTERFACE REDUNDANCY

Avoid redundant arguments in module interfaces unless the redundancy is there for a particular reason, (e.g., for use by defensive-programming checks). Redundant interface data increases the complexity of the interface and often reduces module independence.

As an example, a COBOL module named "edit record" had three input arguments and three output arguments. The input arguments were the record, a counter of valid records, and a counter of invalid records. The output arguments were the two counters and a valid-record switch. The module checked the validity of each field in the record, incremented one of the counters, and then set the valid-record switch.

Clearly the three output items are redundant. Given only one of the three (any one), the calling module could deduce the other two. This unnecessary data complicates the interface and makes "edit record" less independent from its callers.

FUNCTION-INTERFACE CONSISTENCY

Avoid situations where the interface data of a module are not completely consistent with the definition of the module's function. Such situations make the program more difficult to understand because the function description is probably inaccurate. Also, these situations are indications that the module has a lower strength than expected.

As an example, consider a module with the function "convert customer transaction to finance record." One of the output arguments is an excess-balance switch. This switch has no apparent relationship to the module's stated function, so it implies that the module performs the additional function of checking the customer's credit balance against the credit limit. Hence, the real function of the module is "convert customer transaction to finance record and check current credit balance." Since these functions cannot be described coherently as a single higher-level function, the module does not have functional strength as expected; instead, it has communicational strength.

Insure that all input and output data in an interface are pertinent to the module's stated function. If they are not, either they are extraneous and should be eliminated or the module's function should be defined more accurately.

MAXIMUM MODULE FAN-IN

One important goal in designing a well-structured program is to isolate common functions to single modules, rather than implementing the logic for these functions in multiple places. The motivation for this goal should be obvious; it decreases the cost and size of the program and increases its module independence.

In general, the higher the average module fan-in present in a design, the better the design. This is a sign that the designer has exploited module functions in different contexts. It implies that, during the design process, the designer must be aware of the already defined modules to recognize when they can be used in new areas of the design. It also suggests that the definitions of modules may be altered slightly during the design process, for instance, when the designer finds an existing module whose function almost, but not exactly, matches a function needed at another point in the design.

Of course, maximizing module fan-in must not be carried to the point where it decreases module strength or increases module coupling. For instance, logical-strength modules tend to have high fan-ins, but we saw in Chapter 4 that such modules are undesirable.

Another "old wives' tale" in the area of program design that seems to oppose the maximization of fan-in is the belief that a module should only be used at one "level" in the hierarchy. That is, if module A calls B and B calls C, then a call from A to C is prohibited. There is no known technical basis for this tale and it should be disregarded.

RESTRICTIVE MODULES

A restrictive module is one whose function and use have been needlessly restricted either by describing the module incorrectly or by designing "over-specialization" into the module. Restrictive modules should be avoided because they impede changes to the program and reduce the opportunities to reuse the module in multiple contexts in this program and in future programs.

Consider a module with the function "encrypt an 80-character string." This function is probably unnecessarily restricted. Rather than cast the number 80 in concrete, the string size could probably just as easily have been an input argument (or dynamically determined, in a language such as PL/I), which would have made future alterations to the program easier and which would have increased the reuse probability of the module.

Note, however, that this guideline must be applied with adequate judgment because carrying it too far leads to overgenerality of functions and interfaces, thus creating unnecessary complexity.

Restrictive modules also occur when modules are defined in terms of their context of usage rather than their function. Consider a module described as "prompt terminal user for correct password," where the input arguments are a message to be displayed and a terminal address, and where the output argument is the terminal user's reply. It is likely that this module has nothing to do with passwords, so its context of usage has been described rather than its function. The module's true function is described more accurately as "prompt terminal user for reply."

Many stamp-coupled modules are found to be restrictive modules. The VERSAL module in Chapter 5, whose function was "verify reasonableness of employee salary," needed three pieces of input data but was passed a 47-field data structure from which it extracted these data. As was noted in Chapter 5, the module's unnecessary dependence on this data structure severely restricts its usage in other environments.

PREDICTABLE MODULES

A predictable module is one whose function remains constant from one call to another: that is, it is a module that has no "memory" from one call to another. A module that alters a local variable to retain a value between invocations (any variable in COBOL or FORTRAN, a STATIC variable in PL/I) is an unpredictable module.

As an example, a module named "obtain employee data" was defined for a seemingly noble purpose—to hide the format of the employee personnel record from all other modules. The input argument is an employee number and the output argument is the next field in that employee's record. If the employee number is the same as that in the previous invocation, the next successive field in the record is returned; if not, the record for this employee is read from the file and the first field in the record is returned.

The logic of the module keeps three items in static storage across invocations: the current employee number, the record, and a field count. The module is unpredictable because, for any given invocation, the output is unpredictable. The output is dependent upon what happened during the previous call to the module. This module exhibited the following problems, most of which are associated with unpredictable modules.

First, the module cannot be used easily in multiple places in the program.

If module A is in the midst of obtaining the fields for employee X and module B calls the module to obtain the fields for employee Y, then the next call by module A will cause the *first* field of employee X to be returned again. Also, the module is not reentrant.

A second problem is that the interface conventions are complicated. Since the fields have different sizes and attributes, there is no easy way to return the fields directly as output arguments. This forced the programmer to define the output argument as a *pointer* to the field. The calling modules, after each call, base a variable on the pointer. Note that this implies that the calling module must know the attributes of each field, the number of fields, and the precise order of the fields. Hence, the "obtain employee data" module accomplishes absolutely nothing! It does not in any way "hide" the employee record; the calling modules are completely sensitive to the organization of the record. Furthermore, they are sensitive in an undesirable way. Rather than containing a compile-time copy of the record, the *logic* of each calling module is sensitive to the record organization.

Needless to say, a third problem is that the program exhibits extra performance overhead. Furthermore, if more fields are added to the employee records, a corresponding number of additional calls to this module must be added.

Although unpredictable modules are not desirable, their presence is occasionally warranted, but the use of each such module should be carefully justified. It may be desirable in a module named "print next report section" to hide the concept of page ejecting. Thus, this module will have a memory, a lines-printed counter, to be used to determine when to skip to a new printed page. Although this makes the module an unpredictable module, it might be acceptable in this instance.

RECURSION

One additional program-structure term that must be introduced is an *activation* of a module. An activation is an occurrence of a module being in an active state. A module is in an active state if one of the following situations applies:

1. The module is being executed.
2. The module was executing, but execution has been suspended temporarily by the underlying system (e.g., in a multiprogramming system when the system dispatches another program).
3. The module was executing, but execution has been suspended temporarily because this module has called another module.

The pertinent consideration here is determining if it is possible for a module to have multiple activations. The answer is yes; there are two situations in which a module can be in multiple active states simultaneously. The first situation occurs with multitasking or parallel processing, when a module is being executed by parallel tasks or processes. The second situation is that of recursion, when a module is a superordinate and subordinate of itself. The usual appearance of recursion is where a module is an immediate-superordinate and immediate-subordinate of itself; that is, the module calls itself.

Recursion is a powerful program-structuring mechanism under certain circumstances. The two circumstances that must be present to make use of a recursive module desirable are

1. The problem being solved by the module is recursively defined. A recursive problem is one in which one or more subproblems are identical to the problem.
2. The problem is not one-dimensional (linear): that is, back-ups and restarts are necessary in solving the problem.

The traditional example of recursion in programming texts is the factorial function. The factorial function is a recursive problem because it is defined as

$$X! = X\,(X-1)\,! \quad \text{for } X>0$$
$$= 1 \qquad \text{for } X=0$$

However, the factorial problem is a one-dimensional problem. One solves $X!$ by decrementing X and multiplying; there is no need to go back to a previous value of X. Hence, the factorial problem does not warrant a recursive module; it is best solved by iteration (i.e., a DO or PERFORM-UNTIL loop).

Figure 6.1 is an illustration of a problem meeting both criteria. Assume that Figure 6.1 is a bill-of-material tree (a slight misuse of terminology, since bill-of-material "trees" are defined more correctly as lattices or networks). The nodes represent parts and the edges define the parts that are directly included in another part. For instance, part A is constructed from parts B, C, and D; part B is constructed from E and F, and so on.

Consider the problem: given the name of any part in the tree, produce a list of all parts that are subordinate to that part. For instance, given part A, the answer is BCDEFGH. Such a problem satisfies both of the above criteria, implying that a recursive solution (module) is easier than a nonrecursive solution.

Figure 6.1   A bill-of-material network

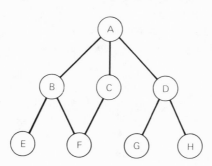

The first criterion is met because the problem of finding all subordinates of A is equivalent to listing B, C, and D, and then finding all subordinates of B, C, and D. Likewise, any one of these subproblems can be subdivided in a similar fashion. The second criterion is met because the problem is not one-dimensional. For instance, after finding the subordinates of B, we must move back up the tree and begin finding the subordinates of C.

Figure 6.2 is a recursive PL/I module that solves this problem. Note the simplicity of the logic; the module contains only five executable statements. A nonrecursive solution would be much more difficult because in the recursive module the compiler, rather than the programmer, takes on the burdens of storage management and backtracking.

Since recursion is a mystery to many people, it is best understood by "playing computer"; in other words, mentally walking a set of data through the module. Initially it is best to assume an infinite supply of identical recursive modules. When walking through EXPLODE, assume that the call statement to EXPLODE calls a physically separate, but identical, version of EXPLODE with its own set of variables. Once this representation of the program is understood, it

Figure 6.2   Recursive bill-of-material module

```
EXPLODE: PROCEDURE(PART,LIST,COUNT,ISCOUNT) RECURSIVE;
/*PLACE IN LIST THE NAMES OF ALL PARTS IN THE TREE SUBORDINATE TO PART.
  COUNT IS THE CURRENT NUMBER OF ENTRIES IN LIST. ISCOUNT IS THE MAXIMUM
  NUMBER OF PARTS THAT ARE IMMEDIATELY SUBORDINATE TO A PART.
  INPUTS: PART,LIST,COUNT,ISCOUNT
  OUTPUTS: LIST,COUNT                              */

DECLARE PART CHARACTER(8),   /*PARAMETERS*/
          LIST (*) CHARACTER(8),
          COUNT FIXED DECIMAL(5),
          ISCOUNT FIXED DECIMAL(5);
DECLARE                             /*LOCAL STORAGE*/
          IMMSUB(ISCOUNT) CHARACTER(8),
          N     FIXED DECIMAL(5),
          I     FIXED DECIMAL(5);
CALL GETIS(PART,IMMSUB,N); /*RETURNS IMMEDIATE
   SUBORDINATE PARTS (AND A COUNT OF THEM) OF PART*/
DO I=1 TO N;
   COUNT=COUNT + 1;
   LIST(COUNT)=IMMSUB(I);
   CALL EXPLODE(IMMSUB(I),LIST,COUNT,ISCOUNT);
END;
END;
```

64

is not difficult to see how a compiler can produce the same effect with only a single copy of the module (by dynamically allocating storage for the local variables on a pushdown stack).

Although any recursive module can also be coded as an equivalent nonrecursive module, recursion simplifies the module's logic and minimizes "wired-in" restrictions and assumptions. Many programming problems (e.g., searches of trees or networks, sorting algorithms, processing nested macros, list processing, game playing, and formula manipulation) are best solved by recursive modules.

EXERCISES

1. Why is it reasonable to expect that the optimal average size should increase for larger programs?

2. The section on interface redundancy stated that the "edit record" module was less independent from its callers because of the counters of valid and invalid records. Why?

3. Is there a function-interface inconsistency in a module that performs the function "get master record" and where one of the output parameters is an error code defined as "no record found"?

4. Is the module "get next input transaction" an unpredictable module?

5. Which of the following problems are good candidates for recursive modules?
   a. Searching an array for an element having a particular value
   b. Finding the terminal modes (the nodes having no subordinate nodes) in a tree
   c. Implementing a sorting algorithm that repeatedly breaks the input list into smaller lists to be individually sorted
   d. Searching a string for a particular substring
   e. Finding a path between two nodes in a graph

6. Does your primary programming language permit recursive modules?

7. Walk the part tree of Figure 6.1 through the recursive module EXPLODE in Figure 6.2.

8. Write a nonrecursive version of the module in Figure 6.2. Why is the nonrecursive version more complicated? Did you introduce any new dependencies (e.g., an assumption about the maximum number of parts in the tree)?

7

The Design Thought-Process

In developing any methodology, two distinct items must be considered. First, the desirable attributes or goals of the result (solution) must be established. Second, methods for the solution process itself must be devised so that when these methods are used the result achieves the defined goals. One can find this distinction in the well-known programming methodology of structured programming. Most people think of structured programming as a set of rules: use only the three basic control constructs (sequence, selection, and iteration), avoid most uses of the GO TO statement, indent the source code to show clearly the flow of execution, use good programming style, and so forth. Note, however, that these factors are the goals; they are measurements of the final result, but they do not give us a *method* to use to achieve these goals. The rules tell us how to recognize a good result, but they tell us little about how to go about the process of designing the logic of a module.

Associated with structured programming is a thought-process called "stepwise refinement." Stepwise refinement is the method for the solution process; one uses stepwise refinement to produce source code that hopefully adheres to the "rules" of structured programming.

A situation analogous to structured programming exists with composite design. The topics of the previous chapters (e.g., module strength and coupling) define the attributes of a well-designed program, but they tell us little about how to go about the process of designing such a program. Therefore, a second major part of composite design is a set of thought-processes. These thought-processes are related to the goals in the previous few chapters in the same way that stepwise refinement is related to the attributes of a structured program.

These thought-processes are iterative, top-down, reasoning processes. That is, one uses them repeatedly, working from the top of the program downwards, to define the entire modular structure of the program (a specification of module functions, module relationships, and module interfaces). The thought-processes also lead the designer, without explicitly thinking about it, to produce a program of high-strength and loosely coupled modules.

It is important to realize at the start that these thought-processes are simply what the term denotes—thought-processes. They are not substitutes for creativity, experience, wisdom, and common sense. Their purpose is to channel the designer's attention in productive directions, but they may need to be altered and adapted to the particular program at hand. It is likely that two equally capable designers will not apply the processes in exactly the same way and will develop two different, but perhaps equally good, designs.

One can find an analogy here to problem-solving methods in general. Although the thought-processes in Polya's excellent book on problem solving are likely to help us solve the problem "find the center of gravity in a homogeneous tetrahedron," the solution still requires some creativity, experience with plane and solid geometry, and insight.[1] It is also likely that two people will not solve the problem in precisely the same way.

This chapter introduces the basic aspects of the thought-processes, and Chapters 8–11 discuss distinct kinds of thought-processes (called decomposition techniques). Chapter 12 illustrates the use of all of the techniques on the design of a fairly sophisticated application program, and Chapter 13 discusses two essential last steps: optimizing or improving the initial design of a program and verifying the correctness and quality of the design.

AN OVERVIEW OF THE PROCESS

The design process begins by defining the top module in the program. The definition of the top module is usually quite trivial because its function is identical to the function of the program. If one is designing a PASCAL compiler, the function of the top module is undoubtedly "compile a PASCAL program to the XYZ machine language." If one is designing a program in an accounts-payable system, the top module may be defined as "apply weekly check receipts to accounts-payable master file." Note that if the purpose of the program cannot be described as a single specific function, the top module will not have functional strength. However, if this is the case, our goal should be to limit the lower strength to only this module.

The next step is to view the function of this module as a problem to be solved. Based on the nature of the problem, one of the following decomposition techniques is selected:

1. Source/transform/sink decomposition
2. Transactional decomposition
3. Functional decomposition

The first method is concerned with breaking a function into subfunctions that acquire, transform, and disperse data. The second breaks a function into "peer" subfunctions. The third is concerned with extracting particular kinds of subfunctions from a function.

After the appropriate decomposition technique is selected and applied, a set of immediate-subordinate modules will have been identified. The next step is to define the interfaces between the top module and each of its subordinates. "Defining the interfaces" means identifying the kinds of input and output information transmitted, but not being concerned with precise physical representations.

Once this is complete, the design has a form similar to that of Figure 7.1. The process is repeated on each terminal module (a module that currently has no subordinates). For instance, we might select module *function2*. The function of this module is viewed as a problem to be solved, a decomposition technique is selected and used, a set of modules that are immediately subordinate to this module are identified, and their interfaces are defined. The process is repeated again on one of these modules, or on modules *function3* and *function4*, and so on. Throughout the entire process the designer must consider the guidelines in Chapters 4–6 and must remain aware of the currently defined modules so that functions within the program are not duplicated. The entire process is outlined in Figure 7.2.

STOPPING

Obviously this iterative process must eventually terminate. If it is carried to the extreme, each terminal module will contain only a single executable statement; such modules are usually, but not always, undesirable.

Figure 7.1   The outcome of a decomposition of function 1

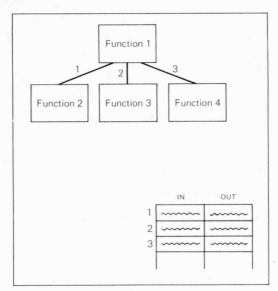

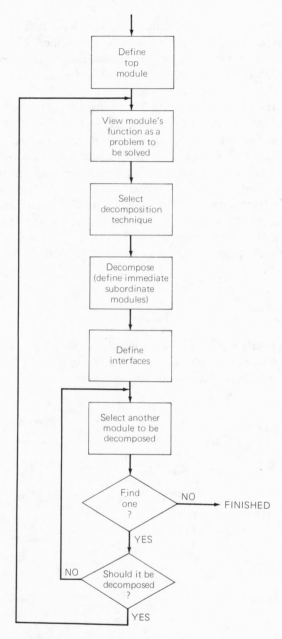

Figure 7.2 The iterative decomposition process

70

The last decision in Figure 7.2 implies that one or more tests should be made on a module before an attempt is made to decompose it. The most useful test is to attempt to visualize the logic of each module before attempting to decompose it. If its logic can be visualized easily, the module will probably contain 50 or less executable statements when coded. Therefore, this is an indication that this module needs no further decomposition and that another module should be selected for decomposition.

A second indication of a stopping point is when a module cannot be decomposed into functional-strength immediate-subordinate modules.

A third way to approach the stopping problem is to use the "banana rule." The banana rule was created by some unknown person who, for some reason, had difficulty spelling the word "banana." Since he had a general idea about the sequence of letters, he would write "bananana . . . ," then step back, pronounce what he had written, and determine how many extra "na" syllables to delete. The analogous situation in program design is: when in doubt, it is better to decompose the program further rather than not far enough. If the decomposition has been excessive, the program can be "undecomposed," either during a review of the completed design or during the process of designing and coding the logic of the individual modules. It is much easier to rectify a program that has been decomposed too far than it is to rectify a program that has been decomposed insufficiently.

TWO PHENOMENA

It is common for someone using this design process to say upon completion, "My design looks reasonable, but I wish I had the chance to redo it because I now *really* see how this program should be designed." There is nothing wrong with such a remark, and it illustrates an effective design technique. Probably the best way to become intimately familiar with a problem is to develop a solution to the problem. That solution may not be optimal, but it is a worthwhile investment because of its educational value. When such a reaction occurs, the designer should be encouraged to either modify the design or completely discard it and start anew. The resultant improvement in the program's design will prove invaluable over the program's lifetime (i.e., contrast a few extra days to redesign a moderate-size program to the many years in which the finished program will evolve and be maintained).

Another effective technique when faced with a large or complicated program is to first design a simpler version of the program. That is, discard all of the exceptional conditions and options, and design a less-complicated version of the program. Once this is done, the designer has two alternatives: depending upon which is more feasible, he can add the additional complexity into the skeletal structure or he can discard the simple design (reaping the educational benefits of understanding the skeletal structure of the program) and redo the program design in its entirety.

REFERENCES

1.   G. Polya, *How to Solve It.* Princeton, N.J.: Princeton University Press, 1971.

8

Source/Transform/Sink Decomposition

The principal decomposition technique of composite design is called STS (source/transform/sink) decomposition. It is the technique that is used first in an attempt to decompose a problem. If this technique is found to be inapplicable, then one of the remaining decomposition techniques is used.

The motivation behind this technique is that every problem has an inherent structure and that the program structure should closely model the problem structure. STS decomposition involves the discovery of the inherent structure of the problem, understanding how data flows through the problem structure, and comprehending how the data is transformed as it moves through the problem structure. This information is used to identify the immediate-subordinate modules of the module being analyzed. The major steps in this decomposition process are

1. Identify and outline the structure of the problem.
2. In this problem structure, identify the major stream of input data and the major stream of output data.
3. Identify the point in the problem structure where the input data stream last exists as a logical entity and the point where the output data stream first exists as a logical entity.
4. Using these points as dividing points in the problem structure, describe each division of the problem as a single function. These become the functions of the immediate-subordinate modules.

These steps are described in more detail in the following sections.

OUTLINE THE PROBLEM STRUCTURE

The first step in STS decomposition is a discovery process—an investigation into the inherent or underlying structure of the problem. The objective is to outline the structure of the problem as a sequence of about three to ten subproblems,

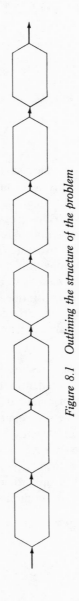

Figure 8.1 Outlining the structure of the problem

```
Execute
all retrieval
requests
```

Figure 8.2   Top module of the information-retrieval system

as illustrated in Figure 8.1. The sequencing of the subproblems is not intended to describe a procedural relationship but instead a *data flow* or *data dependency* relationship. If we view the subproblems as being numbered 1,2, . . . , N, then the subproblems should be ordered so that subproblem i is dependent upon the results of some or all of subproblems 1,2, . . . , $i-1$ and is not dependent upon subproblems $i+1$, . . . , N. If the problem being analyzed cannot be depicted this way, this is a good indication that the problem cannot be decomposed by STS decomposition (i.e., a different decomposition technique must be used).

As an example, consider the design of an information-retrieval system. Ordinarily we would expect to have a detailed specification describing the external, user-oriented, characteristics of the system, but since we are only going to design the top few levels of the system here, a short summary of the specification is sufficient. The system contains a data base of documents in which each record contains the document's title, author, date, periodical title or report number, a set of keywords describing the content of the document, and an index to the document's abstract. The system also contains a file of abstracts of these documents. A user can type a retrieval request such as "find all papers published prior to 1955 on microprogramming *or* computer control units *and* logic arrays." The system will respond by displaying all applicable abstracts at the terminal.

Since we are beginning the program's design, the top module would already be defined as noted in Chapter 7. Therefore, the top module is given in Figure 8.2. What we are attempting to do now is to view this module's function as a problem to be solved and to use STS decomposition to decompose this module.

The problem structure is outlined in Figure 8.3. The first process in the problem is the acquisition of a terminal request. Since the terminal input is hopefully defined in a "humanized" form (i.e., for good human factors), it is probably quite unpalatable for direct use for searching the data base; therefore, another major part of the problem is transforming the user request into a search argument or mask for use with the keyword data base. The remaining problem parts are searching the keyword data base, extracting the abstracts, and displaying the results. The order of the processes depicts the data flow through the problem;

Figure 8.3   Structure of the problem "execute all retrieval requests"

that is, each process or subproblem is dependent on only the processes listed on its left for the data it needs.

IDENTIFY MAJOR DATA STREAMS

After outlining the problem structure, the second step in the STS decomposition process is the identification of the major input and output data streams in the problem. A *data stream* is a logical collection of information; it is independent of any physical representation or physical input/output device. In fact, when we are analyzing a subproblem in the middle of the program, a data stream may be completely independent of input/output operations. It may be an intermediate form of data that only exists within the program.

The first task is to identify the distinct kinds of information entering the problem. If only one is found, this is identified as the major input stream. If multiple input streams are found, then one of them must be identified as the major input stream. This is done by determining which stream of data is the active driving-force of the problem.

Similarly, the distinct kinds of information leaving the problem (the output data streams) must be found. If there are more than one, then the *major* output stream must be selected. This is done by determining which output stream is most closely allied with the function or purpose of the problem. The major input and output data streams are then noted on the problem structure, as in Figure 8.4.

The information-retrieval example appears to have three input streams: the terminal requests, the keyword data base, and the abstract file. Clearly the first is the major input stream; the latter two have a passive role and are used during the problem solution. Let us assume that the system has two distinct output streams: in addition to displaying the results of the retrieval, it also records the input transactions on a journal to allow the installation management to analyze usage of the system. Clearly the former is the major output stream. The purpose of the problem (the module being decomposed) is to do information retrieval; producing a journal is a secondary effect.

The major input and output streams are identified in Figure 8.5. They are named so that no physical representations or forms are implied.

FIND POINTS OF HIGHEST ABSTRACTION

The third step in STS decomposition is the identification of two points in the problem structure which divide the problem into three subproblems. These points are identified in such a way that they split the problem into its most independent subproblems and so that each subproblem can be defined as a single specific function.

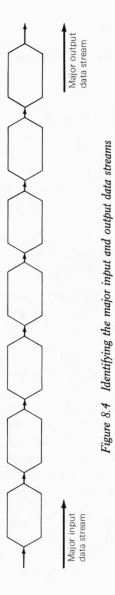

Major input
data stream

Major output
data stream

Figure 8.4   Identifying the major input and output data streams

Figure 8.5   Major input and output data streams of the problem "execute all retrieval requests"

To find the first point, position yourself at the beginning of the problem structure and mentally move into the problem structure, watching the major input data stream as you do so. Two phenomena should be observed:

1. The major input data stream becomes more and more abstract the further you move into the problem structure (where "abstract" means different from its form at the beginning of the problem structure).
2. A point will be found beyond which the major input stream does not seem to exist (or beyond which the major input stream exists but it is no longer useful for the primary purpose of the problem).

The point to look for is the point where the input stream is in its most abstract form. This is the last point in the problem structure where the input stream is still distinguishable as a useful logical entity (perhaps point *c* in Figure 8.6).

The same process is used to find the second point, but by analysis of the major output stream. Start at the end of the problem structure and back-up into the problem, watching the major output stream as you do so. The output stream should appear in a more abstract form the further you back into the problem; eventually a point will be found where the major output stream first appears as a logical entity (perhaps point *e* in Figure 8.6).

The premise is 1) that these two "points of highest abstraction" divide the problem into its three most independent subproblems and 2) that these subproblems can be defined as single specific functions.

The two points can now be found in the example shown in Figure 8.7. The input stream (retrieval requests) obviously exists at point *a*. It also exists at point *b*. Furthermore, the retrieval-request stream is also present at point *c*, but in a more abstract form because it has been transformed into a search query for the data base. It does not seem to exist at point *d* or beyond; therefore, point *c* is identified as the first point.

To clarify a possible point of confusion, the input stream in this example is probably carried through the program to point *f* so that the user's original request is displayed with his results. However, we disregard this in finding the point of highest abstraction. Point *c* is both the last place where the input stream is useful

78

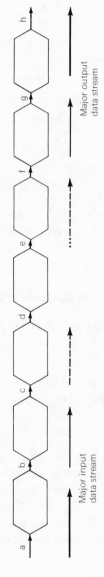

Figure 8.6 Locating the points of highest abstraction

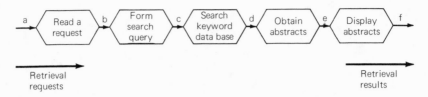

Figure 8.7 Locating the points of highest abstraction in the problem "execute all retrieval requests"

to the major purpose of the problem and the last place where the input stream exists as a distinct entity. Because of these considerations, it is defined as the first point of highest abstraction.

To find the second point, the output stream (retrieval results) obviously exists at points *f* and *e*. However, a highly abstract form of the output stream is apparent at point *d*. At point *d* we have some type of list of the applicable abstracts. Although the abstracts, not this list, are the final physical output, there is a direct one-to-one correspondence between the list items and the abstracts. Therefore, *d* is considered the point of highest abstraction of the output stream.

DEFINE IMMEDIATE-SUBORDINATE MODULES

In contrast to the previous step, the last step is quite simple. The two points have broken the problem into *source, transform,* and *sink* functions that can be described generically as

1. Acquire the major input data stream in its most abstract form
2. Transform the major input data stream into the major output data stream in its most abstract form
3. Disperse the major output stream

The three pieces of the problem are now described as single specific functions, and three modules having these functions are defined as the immediate-subordinate modules. If one or more pieces of the problem cannot be described as a single function, this is an indication that either the points of highest abstraction were identified incorrectly, this decomposition technique is not applicable to this problem, or the problem is slightly peculiar and this decomposition technique must be adapted to it.

The results of the decomposition of the example are shown in Figure 8.8. Note that before another iterative decomposition is started, the interfaces must be defined. Module "get next search query" has no input arguments and four outputs: the search query to be used against the data base, the user's retrieval

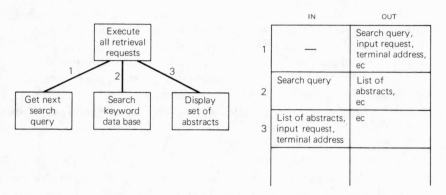

	IN	OUT
1	—	Search query, input request, terminal address, ec
2	Search query	List of abstracts, ec
3	List of abstracts, input request, terminal address	ec

Figure 8.8 Decomposition of "execute all retrieval requests"

command, an identification of the user's terminal, and a yet-to-be-defined error code.* The identification of the remaining two interfaces is straightforward.

MODIFICATIONS OF THE TECHNIQUE

As was mentioned in Chapter 7, the decomposition techniques are not "cookbook" approaches to design; they often must be modified in certain situations. One such situation is where one cannot validly designate one of several input or output streams as the *major* stream. In this case the problem structure might have to be redrawn as shown in Figure 8.9, where the first problem is one that has two primary input streams and the second problem is an example of one with

*Since virtually every module in every program may encounter some error that prohibits it from performing its function, automatically giving every module an error-code output is a good idea.

Figure 8.9 Situations of multiple major input or output streams

81

two primary output streams. In these cases more than two points of highest abstraction are found. For instance, in the first diagram, one point is located for each of the two input streams and for the major output stream; thus, the problem is broken into four parts and, subsequently, into four subordinate modules.

There are also situations where the two points fall at the same place, thus breaking the problem into two pieces. This occurs in problems that contain no transform between input and output streams, for example, the problem "copy file X into file Y."

The motivation behind finding the points of highest abstraction is to discover how to partition the problem into its most independent subproblems. Knowing that this is the motivation can be of assistance if difficulty is encountered in either locating the major input and output streams or in finding their points of apperance and disappearance. In other words, one can adopt an alternative method by simply examining the problem structure and partitioning it, in an ad hoc way, into what appear to be the most independent sets of subproblems.

Although STS decomposition can be applied at any level of the program structure, its use may have to be altered depending on what type of module is being decomposed (i.e., source, transform, or sink module). For instance, if the source module "build edited input file for sort" is being decomposed, it is likely to have source, transform, and sink subordinates. However, if the source module returns its data stream directly to its caller, then it may not have a sink (data dispersing) subordinate, *because the sink subproblem is located within the module (a source module) itself.* Decomposition of the source module "get next search query" will illustrate this. The problem represented by this module is shown in Figure 8.10. The major input and output data streams of this problem and their points of highest abstraction are also shown. However, module "get next search query" would be defined with only two subordinates: "read next valid retrieval request" and "convert valid retrieval request to search query." The subproblem "return search query" is solved in the logic of module "get next search query."

Similarly, this situation occurs in sink modules. If a sink module receives its input stream indirectly (e.g., the module "produce listing from file PAYREC"), we might expect it to have a source immediate-subordinate module. However, if the module receives its input stream directly (e.g., the module "display error

Figure 8.10   Analysis of the problem "get next search query"

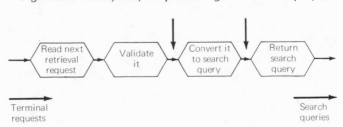

message on screen"), it probably will not have a source subordinate.

Both of the above situations apply for transform modules. All of these situations can be accounted in the following guidelines:

1. All functions (problems) consist of source, transform, and sink subfunctions (subproblems).
2. If a source (data acquisition) module returns its output stream indirectly, it is likely to have a sink subordinate. Otherwise the sink subfunction resides in the logic of the source module.
3. If a sink (data dispensation) module obtains its input stream indirectly, it is likely to have a source subordinate. Otherwise the source subfunction resides in the logic of the sink module.
4. If a transform module obtains its input stream indirectly, it is likely to have a source subordinate; otherwise, the source subfunction resides in the logic of the transform module.
5. If a transform module returns its output stream indirectly, it is likely to have a sink subordinate; otherwise, the sink subfunction resides in the logic of the transform module.

EXERCISES

A professional basketball team is developing a set of programs to assist its scouting of collegiate players. One of these programs is to store scouting reports in a direct-access file and to print a report of the players that need immediate scouting attention.

The input transactions are scouting reports. A transaction contains an athlete's name (12 characters), school (12 characters), name of the scout (12 characters), date (6 characters), the scout's numerical rating of the athlete (1 decimal digit), and a 100-character free-format textual report. The direct-access file contains two types of records. An athlete record contains the athlete's name, school, the average of the numerical ratings of all scouting reports, a numerical field indicating the number of scouting reports for that athlete, and other information. Athlete records can be accessed serially or directly (by a search key consisting of the athlete's name and school).

Each athlete record points to a chain of zero or more scouting records. The fields in a scouting record are the scout's name, date, numerical rating, and the textual report. Figure 8.11 illustrates the format of these records and the input transaction.

The program reads scouting reports from a terminal and uses these to update the file. For each scouting report, the program creates a scouting record, adds this to the chain of scouting records for that athlete, and updates the average-rating and number-of-reports fields in the athlete's record.

When the terminal user enters a blank line, the program produces a report of those athletes that warrant immediate scouting attention. These athletes are defined as

1. Athletes with zero scouting reports.

2. The 10 athletes with average ratings above one and the fewest scouting reports. If there are additional athletes with the same number of reports as the tenth athlete, then these athletes are included as well.

83

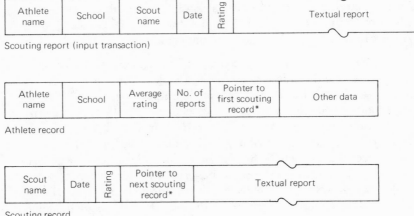

Figure 8.11   Record and input transaction formats

The input transactions are entered from a terminal. Any errors encountered (e.g., incorrect format, athlete not in file) are reported to the terminal user.

1. Define the top module in this program.

2. Outline the problem structure of the top module.

3. Identify the major input and output data streams.

4. Find the points of highest abstraction.

5. Define the top module's immediate subordinate modules and their interfaces.

6. Outline the problem structures of these immediate-subordinate modules, identify their major input and output streams, and find the points of highest abstraction in each.

7. Decompose the program until you can visualize the logic of each module. Draw a structure chart of the program and define all interfaces.

8. Identify the data structures in the solution to problem 7 that have the potential of creating stamp coupling.

9. Identify all occurrences of stamp coupling in the solution to problem 7.

9

Transactional Decomposition

Unfortunately not all modules can be decomposed with source/transform/sink decomposition. One such module might have the function "apply next transaction to master file." If the module receives distinct types of transactions, and if each type of transaction implies something different about what should be done with the master file, then a linear problem structure cannot be drawn for this module. The module is a *data-driven* module; it performs a distinct set of operations for each transaction type. That is, the problem structure has the form of a selection process, and transactional decomposition is the appropriate way to decompose the module.

Consider a module with the function "apply next merchandise transaction to merchandise file" in a program that keeps track of the inventory of a store. Assume there are six types of merchandise transactions: sale, return, incoming shipment, outgoing shipment to another store, addition of a new item of merchandise, and discontinuance of an item. Source/transform/sink decomposition will not work for this module because the problem cannot be depicted as a fixed sequence of subproblems. Hence, we use transactional decomposition; the module is decomposed into a set of subordinate modules, each performing the function of applying a single type of transaction to the merchandise file as shown in Figure 9.1.

Note how this simple, and almost obvious, decomposition injects independence into the program. For instance, the "apply sale transaction to file" module is the only module aware of the syntax and semantics of a sale transaction. Furthermore, this module knows absolutely nothing of the other transaction types. Module "apply merchandise transaction to file" knows the possible types of transactions, but it knows nothing of the syntax and semantics of each transaction.

As was noted in Chapter 7, an appropriate decomposition technique is selected for each problem being analyzed, and one use of a decomposition technique does not imply anything about what decomposition techniques will be used elsewhere in the program. For instance, the use of transactional decomposition to arrive at Figure 9.1 does not imply that we should use transactional

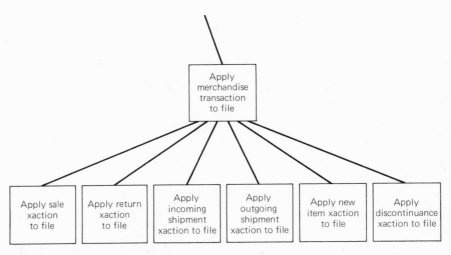

Figure 9.1 A transactional decomposition of the problem "apply merchandise transaction to file"

decomposition on the subordinate modules as well. In fact it is likely that one would find source/transform/sink decomposition most applicable in decomposing "apply sale transaction to file" and its five peers.

The above form of transactional decomposition is used when the input stream is transmitted directly. However, when the input stream is transmitted indirectly (i.e., the module being decomposed must obtain the input stream from some external source), a two-level transactional decomposition, as modeled in Figure 9.2, is used. That is, the problem is subdivided into two functions that

Figure 9.2 Transactional decomposition model when the input stream is indirectly obtained

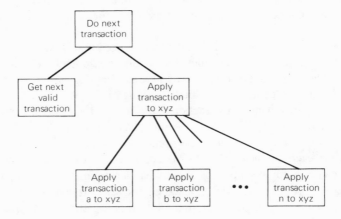

obtain a transaction and deal with the transaction. The latter function is then decomposed into functions that are peculiar to each transaction type.

EXERCISES

1. Which of the following problems seem best served by transactional decomposition?
   a. Update scouting file with next scouting report
   b. Parse a PL/I statement
   c. Execute next editor subcommand
   d. Display set of abstracts
   e. Execute next job-control-language statement
   f. Print designated sales report

10

Functional Decomposition

The third and simplest type of decomposition is functional decomposition. Functional decomposition is an ad hoc process of pulling single subfunctions (i.e., defining immediate-subordinate modules) from a module to achieve certain purposes. These purposes are usually

1. Isolating common functions (If a group of modules are found to contain a common subfunction, it is often desirable to remove the subfunction and define it as a separate module.)
2. Isolating functions within informational-strength modules

To illustrate the second circumstance, assume we have a group of modules that are sensitive to a particular data structure. Normally we could discard these modules and replace them with a single informational-strength module, thus hiding the data structure within a single module. However, assume the program contains two data structures and we wish to hide each of them in two informational-strength modules. A dilemma arises if one of the current modules references *both* structures. To resolve this we could use functional decomposition on this module: draw the module's problem structure, find those subfunctions that reference each data structure, and withdraw these subfunctions as two immediate-subordinate modules. These two immediate-subordinate modules can then be replaced by an entry point in each informational-strength module.

As an example, assume we have a module "build table of underpaid employees." The module sequentially examines the personnel file and, if an employee meets the underpaid criteria, it places the employee in the table. A table entry contains the employee's name, department number, and salary. Assume that the module was not decomposed further because its logic is easily visualized, but we now desire to create informational-strength modules for the personnel records and the "underpaid" table. The first step is drawing the module's problem structure as in Figure 10.1.

We can now distinguish two subfunctions that reference only one structure each: obtain the salary fields for the next employee and add an employee to the

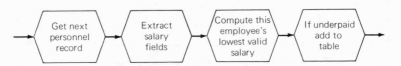

Figure 10.1 Structure of the problem "build table of underpaid employees"

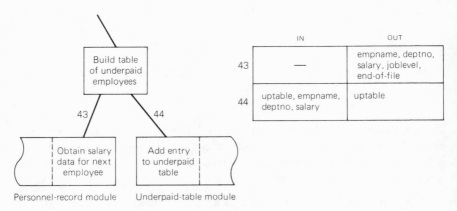

Figure 10.2 Functional decomposition of "build table of underpaid employees"

underpaid table. These functions are removed from the module and added to the informational-strength modules as shown in Figure 10.2.

EXERCISES

1. Given that this chapter is very short, why was it written as a separate chapter? That is, why wasn't this material placed in a previous chapter?

2. Use functional decomposition on the "add scouting record to file" module in exercise 7 of Chapter 8 to eliminate the module's stamp coupling via the athlete record.

11

Data Structure Decomposition

Source/transform/sink decomposition was based on an analysis of *data flow* through a problem. However, one could also envision an alternative technique in which the analysis is not based on data flow but on the *data structure* of the input and output streams. This chapter summarizes such a technique contributed by Jackson.[1] It is not clear at this time how this technique relates to the decomposition methods in the previous chapters, but it is described here to familiarize the reader with the ideas and perhaps to encourage the reader to explore the integration of this technique with the ideas in prior chapters.

The decomposition technique proposed by Jackson is based on the premise that the program's structure should reflect the correspondences between the structures of the input and output data of the program. The four steps in doing this are

1. Record your understanding of the problem environment by defining the structures of the input and output data.
2. Find one-to-one relationships between components of these data structures. If this cannot be done, certain intermediate data structures are defined.
3. Form a program structure based on these relationships.
4. Allocate the elementary operations (program statements) to the appropriate components of the program structure.

When Jackson uses the term "program structure," he means "program logic structure." That is, this technique is primarily oriented towards the design of the program logic; it is not directly concerned with drawing module boundaries and defining module interfaces. However, step 3 identifies segments of program logic, and these segments are defined in functional terms, so the technique does appear to give the designer some insight into desirable module boundaries.

The technique restricts one's thinking to four types of components: elementary, sequence, iteration, and selection. These component types apply to data as well as program logic. This is of special significance because it provides the insight of how to derive program structures from structures of data.

An *elementary* component is an atomic component (the other three are collective components); it is something that cannot be dissected further. For example, an elementary program component is a single statement and an elementary data component is a single data item or field.

A *sequence* component is a component that has more than one part, each appearing only once and in order. A PL/I or COBOL *structure* (e.g., a record containing a sequence of fields) is a data sequence. A set of statements that is entered only at the first statement and exits only at the last statement is a program logic sequence.

An *iteration* component has a single part that occurs zero or more times. An array and a set of records on a sequential file are examples of data iterations. A program iteration is a DO or PERFORM loop.

A *selection* component has more than one part, only one of which is present in each occurrence of the selection component. A data area that, at any instant, can hold a credit, debit, or transfer transaction is an example of a selection data component. An IFTHENELSE or CASE statement is a selection logic component.

These components are expressed in a notation as illustrated in Figure 11.1. A is a sequence of components B, C, and D. E is an iteration of part F. G is a selection whose parts (components) are H, I, J, and K. Sequence, iteration, or selection is indicated by a character (or absence thereof) in the upper-right corner of the components. It is important to recognize that this notation is used to describe both data and program structures.

Figure 11.1   Sequence, iteration, and selection components

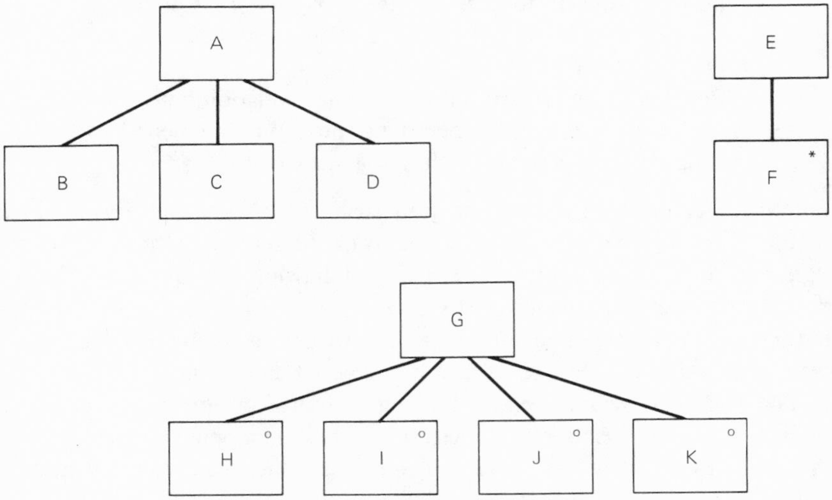

Note that these structures may be combined and nested. We could describe a file as a sequence of a header record and an iteration of transaction records, where a transaction record is a selection of credit, debit, and transfer records.

To illustrate this design technique, we can study an example adapted from Jackson. [1] The program summarizes records of customer payments on an input file. The file, sorted by customer number, contains payment records and other record types that should be ignored by the program. A payment record contains the identifier PR, a customer number, and the date and amount of the payment. The report lists all payment records, totals of all payments by a single customer, and a final line totaling all payments on the input file.

The data structures for the program's input and output are shown in Figure 11.2. The input file is an iteration of customer groups. A customer group is an iteration of records for a single customer. A customer record is a selection of either a payment record or another record type. The payment report is a sequence of the report header, the report body, and the final-total line. The report body is an iteration of customer payment reports. A customer payment report is a sequence of the customer report body and the customer-total line. A customer report body is an iteration of payment-record lines.

The next step is to find the one-to-one relationships between the two structures as shown in Figure 11.3. There is one payment report per input file, one

Figure 11.2   The input and output data structures

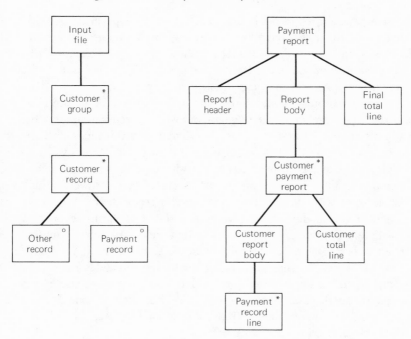

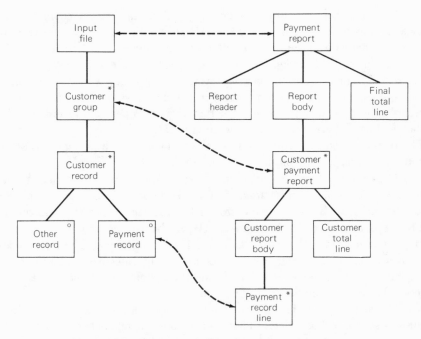

Figure 11.3 Discovery of the one-to-one correspondences

customer payment report per customer group, and one payment-record line per payment record. If the mapping was perfect, the program structure would be identical to the output data (report) structure. However, the third relationship is between an iteration and selection component; hence, we must reflect this selection component in the program structure.

The derived program structure is shown in Figure 11.4. Figure 11.4 represents the *logic structure* of the program, but we are interested in identifying the program's *module structure*. This is a shortcoming of this method; the module structure is not obvious. Let us begin by assuming that each box is a module. Module "print final-total line" needs the total-payments amount as an input; therefore, this must be an output of "print report body." However, this output is inconsistent with the function of printing a report body. Accordingly, the function of the module is more accurately stated as "print report body and calculate total payments," but this implies that the module has communicational strength at best. One can find similar situations elsewhere in Figure 11.4. As was stated in Chapter 7, arriving at a set of low-strength modules is a sign that the decomposition has been carried too far. Based upon this premise, it might be assumed that perhaps each box is not a module. Furthermore, one can find a lack of independence among many of the boxes; for instance, four of the boxes perform physical print operations.

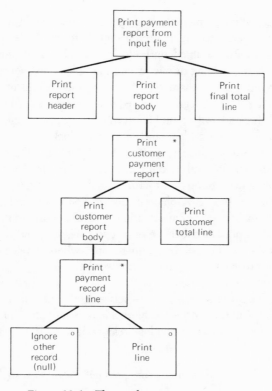

Figure 11.4   The resultant program structure

The idea of identifying the inherent structures of the input and output data and then organizing the program along these lines is appealing. In fact, the value of this technique to design *logic* seems sound, but how the technique is used to partition a program into a hierarchy of modules is an open question. For example, since the logic of the example program can be easily visualized, we might decide that it should be a single-module program and use this design technique to produce the structured code for this module.

STRUCTURE CLASHES

The process of finding one-to-one correspondences between the data structures is fundamental to Jackson's technique. It is this property that allows one to find a single program structure that fits both data structures. However, one is often faced with the situation where the one-to-one correspondence does not exist. When this is the case, a *structure clash* is said to occur. In such an instance, intermediate data structures are introduced to resolve the problem.

Jackson uses a telegram-analysis program to illustrate this situation. The version presented below has been altered slightly to eliminate some ambiguity. The input file contains variable-length blocks. Each block contains a number of words—a word being a string of one or more nonblank characters that is delimited by one or more blank characters, the start and/or end of a block, or the special word "ZZZZ." A telegram is a sequence of words followed by the word "ZZZZ." Each file ends with a null (zero words) telegram. Telegrams may start and end anywhere within a block and may span blocks.

The program is to produce a report that lists, for each telegram, the number of words in the telegram and a count of oversize (greater than 12 characters) words. The input and output data structures are shown in Figure 11.5. A telegram file is an iteration of blocks. A block is an iteration of character groups, and a character group is a selection of an iteration of blanks or an iteration of nonblank characters. The output is a sequence of a report heading and report body. The report body is an iteration of telegram reports, where a telegram report is a sequence of a word count and an oversize-word count.

The problem with Figure 11.5 is that the one-to-one relationships do not seem to exist. There is a relationship between a telegram file and the telegram reports, but the similarity ends here. There is no correspondence between a block and a report on an individual telegram; a telegram can span blocks

Figure 11.5   Telegram program input and output data structures

96

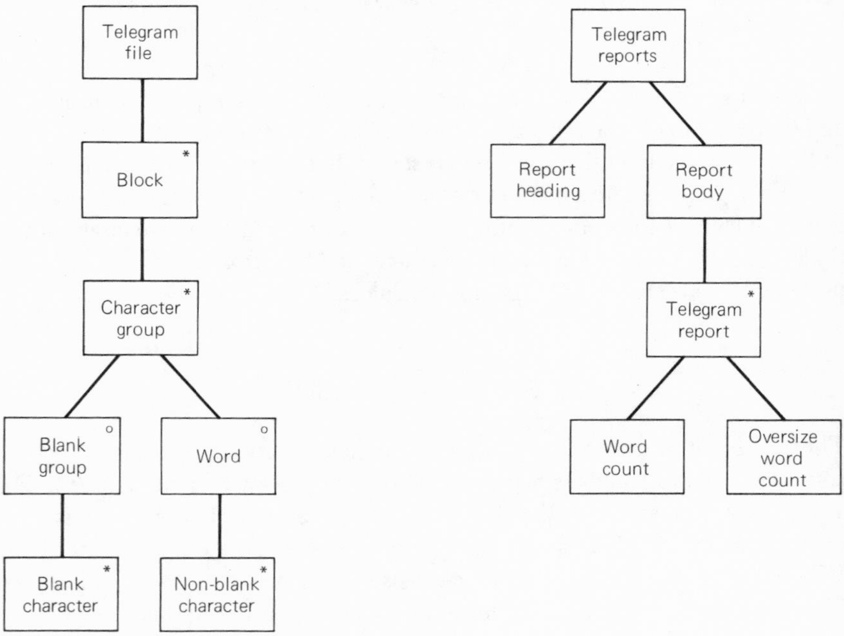

and a block can contain multiple telegrams. Hence, a structure clash exists.

The way to begin resolving this clash is to realize that *two* programs could be used: one that knows about blocks and one that knows about telegrams. Blocks and telegrams have one attribute in common; both consist of an integral number of words. Therefore, we can construct an intermediate data structure—a sequence of words. Thus the first program will read the input file and convert it to an intermediate file having one word per record. The second program will read the intermediate file and produce the report. Note that the final program will not contain this intermediate file; visualizing it is just a step in the design process.

The structure of the intermediate file is shown in Figure 11.6. Notice that the two programs view the file differently. Although they both use the same file, they do not interpret its content in a similar manner. The first program has the left view of the file: an iteration of words. The second program has the rightmost view of the file: it sees the file as a sequence of an iteration of telegrams followed by a null telegram (a telegram is an iteration of words followed by a ZZZZ word, and a word is a selection of a normal or oversize word).

Figure 11.6 Two views of the structure of the intermediate file

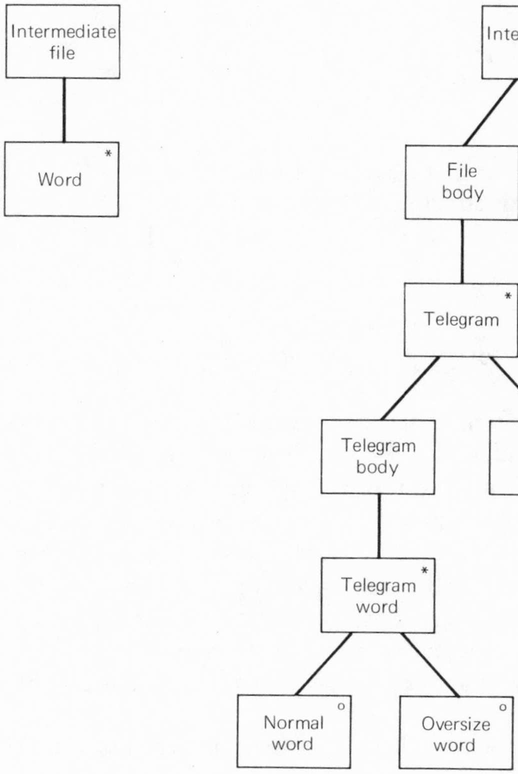

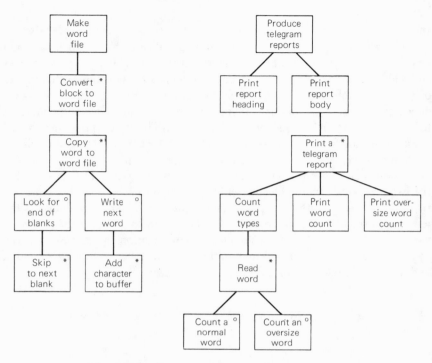

Figure 11.7   Structure of the two telegram programs

We can now easily see a one-to-one correspondence from the left structure of Figure 11.6 to the left structure of Figure 11.5 and from the right structure of Figure 11.5 to the right structure of Figure 11.6. The two programs are structured in Figure 11.7.

PROGRAM INVERSION

Although the use of intermediate files resolves the structure clashes, it adds obvious inefficiencies and is also conceptually unnecessary. If there was a way to multiprogram (concurrently execute) and synchronize the two programs, the intermediate file would be unnecessary. This is because the first program sequentially writes the file and the second program sequentially reads it. Therefore, the file could then be replaced with a single-record buffer. Whenever the first program would have written a record, it would wait until the buffer is empty and then place the record in the buffer; whenever the second program would have read a record, it would wait until a record is placed into the buffer and then move it out and process it.

Once we convince ourselves that the two programs can work successfully this way, we can achieve the same effect, without the buffer and the multiprogramming, by directly linking the programs. This is done by "inverting" one of the programs and having the other program call it. Inverting a program does not substantially change its function but does, in a sense, invert its function. In the telegram-analysis example, we could invert the first program by changing its function to "obtain next word." Every "read from the file" in the second program would be changed to a call to "obtain next word" (i.e., a call upon the first program). Every "write to the file" in the first program would be changed to a "return to the second program."

The programs could also be inverted the other way: by inverting the second program. The function of the second program would be redefined as "use next word in production of telegram reports." Every "write to the file" in the first program would be changed to a call to "use next word in production of telegram reports." Every "read from the file" in the second (inverted) program would be changed to a "return to the first program."

Unfortunately program inversion is not as simple as it first appears. If the inverted program contains "reads" or "writes" for the intermediate file at multiple places within its logic, the simple changes described above will not work correctly. This is because, when the inverted program is reactivated, execution will not resume at the point of return (where the read or write used to be); instead, it will resume at the initial entry point. This suggests that the two programs should be *coroutines*. A coroutine is a module whose point of entry varies—the point of entry being the statement following the last executed statement (which would have been a call to another coroutine). If coroutines were used, the first program would call "use next word in production of telegram reports" whenever it would have written a record. The second program would call "obtain next record" whenever it would have read a record from the intermediate file. When one of the programs is called, it begins execution at the statement after the last call to the other program. Hence, if we used coroutines for both telegram-analysis programs, we have "inverted" both programs.

Although it is easy to create the coroutine linkage mechanism in assembly-language programs, the concept does not exist in the widely used high-level languages. To overcome this, Jackson's technique involves inverting only one of the programs and simulating the coroutine concept in the inverted program by having the program maintain a "state vector." That is, the inverted program "remembers" where it should resume execution (e.g., by using an integer variable in COBOL or a static variable in PL/I); whenever the inverted program is called, it begins with a GO TO (GO TO DEPENDING ON in COBOL) to branch to the appropriate point of resumption.*

Besides the preceding difficulty, program inversion presents us with another

*This mechanism is too complicated to be explained here and one must inspect the logic of the two programs in Figure 11.7 to determine where the programs are linked together; the reader is referred to Chapter 8 of Jackson's book.

problem. The inverted program must return to the other program wherever it has a need to read or to write to or from the intermediate file. This poses a problem if these points are not in the initial module of the inverted program. It violates the convention that "every module returns to its calling module." To avoid this problem, either all the intermediate file operations would have had to exist in the top module (which is unlikely), or the inverted program would have to be defined as a single module (and without any internal subroutines). Jackson recommends the latter approach, but this contradicts all of the prior ideas of composite design since the inverted program is now a large monolithic program.

In summary, the concept of data structure decomposition presents some interesting ideas, but its relationship to the thoughts in the previous 10 chapters is rather fuzzy at this time. The concept was presented here to expose the reader to the ideas and to encourage more thinking about the integration of this technique with those in the previous chapters. One possibility is to use STS, transactional, and functional decomposition to design the module structure of the program and then to use the ideas in this chapter to design the logic of each module. At the least, since the coroutine concept eliminates the problems discussed above, language designers might be motivated to consider adding such a mechanism to the popular high-level languages.

REFERENCES

1. M. A. Jackson, *Principles of Program Design.* London: Academic Press, 1975.

12

A Decomposition Example

The second best way to complete one's understanding of the decomposition techniques in Chapters 7–10 is to follow their use on a realistic example. (The best way to understand them, of course, is to use them yourself.) This chapter illustrates the use of the techniques on a realistic average-size application program. This particular program has proven to be especially valuable because it shows that the decomposition techniques are not "cookbook" approaches; a significant amount of adaptation and thought is required for the design of this program.

THE ENVIRONMENT

The Hypotronics company (a fictitious company) is in the business of designing and manufacturing a wide range of electronic equipment and components. Hypotronics produces standard products (listed in a catalog) and customized equipment and components. Because of the small size and flexibility of the company, Hypotronics emphasizes the customized equipment business.

The company deals with four categories of parts: assembled parts, machined parts, outside parts, and raw materials. An assembled part is produced on an assembly line and can consist of other assembled parts, machined parts, and/or outside parts. A machined part is produced on a machine and can consist of other machined parts, outside parts, and/or raw materials. An outside part is a part purchased from a supplier. Hypotronics views outside parts as "black boxes," that is, it has no knowledge of their "insides." Examples of assembled parts are calculators, signal generators, and signal generator cabinets. Examples of machined parts are gas panels, integrated circuits, and plastic knobs. Parts such as wire, batteries, and integrated circuits are examples of outside parts. Raw materials are such substances as silicon, plastic, gold, carbon, and glass. Certain assembled and machined parts are designated as *products*. A product is a part that is sold over the counter (i.e., it is not customized). Figure 12.1

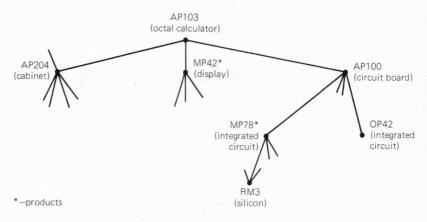

Figure 12.1 Part of the bill-of-material for the construction of part AP103

shows a few of these relationships for the composition of a customized calculator.

Each assembly line and machine has a start-up cost and a per-minute opera-tion cost. For instance, producing nine P404 parts which take two minutes each to manufacture on a machine with a start-up cost of $1000 and a per-minute cost of $5 results in a cost of $1090, *plus* the costs of the parts needed to make nine P404 parts.

To give you a rough idea of the magnitude of Hypotronics' business, it currently deals with 950 distinct parts, 80 of which are products. There are 30 machine types and 10 different assembly lines. The size of the average part (bill-of-material) tree is three levels and 20 items (20 subordinate parts). The largest part tree currently has eight levels and 566 items.

THE PROBLEM

Hypotronics has a manual costing system, a way of calculating the cost of any part. This has become unmanageable because of the large number of parts, the rapid turnover of part types due to the customizing nature of the business and changes in technology, and the volatility of prices (raw material and outside part prices change almost weekly). To alleviate these problems, an automated costing system is needed with the following capabilities upon request:

1. Calculate the current cost of a part.
2. Produce a report showing the current cost of each product.
3. For any part, determine the other parts in which this part is used (a "where-used" function).
4. Determine the parts used in a given part (a "what-used" function).
5. Provide a hypothesizing capability so that a user can add new parts

or change the information associated with a part without affecting the "real" data base, and then use capabilities 1, 3, and 4 above. For instance one might want to hypothesize that the price of silicon increases to four dollars per unit and then determine the resultant cost of part AP103. One might also want to define the structure of a proposed part to determine its cost.

There is an existing parts data base, called DBO, maintained by another department in Hypotronics. Modules that access this data base are available from this other department. There are also n similar data bases called DB1 through DBn. These data bases are initially empty and are used to contain the hypotheses (i.e., hypothesis 4 is stored in DB4). The costing program has authorization to read from DBO and read or write in DB1 through DBn (i.e., when creating or changing a hypothesis).

When the hypothesis capability is being used, the parts data base DBO is concatenated to the hypothesis data base (DBx). This has the following effect. When a read operation is performed on the pair, DBx is searched first. If the record (a part record) exists in DBx, it is returned from there. If not, DBO is searched for the record.

Figure 12.2 shows the format of a part record and indicates which fields are applicable to each type of part. A record for a machined or assembled part contains a variable-length field that lists the parts that are immediately subordinate to (directly used in) this part and the quantity of each immediately subordinate part needed to produce one part (the part described by the record).

Two other data bases are the machine data base DBM and the assembly-line data base DBA. Their records are retrieved by using a machine or assembly-line number as a search key. The records contain the start-up cost and per-minute operating cost of the machine or assembly line.

Figure 12.2   Definition of the part record

	Part number	Unit cost	Type	Product flag	Immed. subordinates (part no., quantity)	Machining (machine, minutes)	Assembly (line, minutes)
Raw material	x	x	x				
Outside part	x	x	x				
Machined part	x		x	x	x, y	x	
Assembled part	x		x	x	x, y		x

x–Field is applicable to this type of part
y–There are multiple occurrences of this
   field (i.e., one for each immediate-subordinate
   part).

THE EXTERNAL SPECIFICATION

Normally one would expect to have a complete and precise external (user-oriented) specification before starting the structural design of the program. However, to conserve space and time, we will take certain liberties and start with an incomplete specification. Obvious omissions from this specification are definitions of error messages and the format of the program's output.

The costing program will be an interactive command-driven program (e.g., it might execute as a foreground application under an IBM OS/VS2 TSO, VM/370 CMS, or similar system). The PARTCOST command activates the costing program. The user can then issue any or all of six subcommands. One of these subcommands is HYPOTHESIS, which places the program in "hypothesis mode" and allows the user to issue any or all of six hypothesis subcommands.

PARTCOST Subcommands

COMPUTECOST PART (number) QUANTITY (number)

This command computes the unit cost of part "number" when produced in quantity "number" and prints this value on the terminal. It assumes that Hypotronics maintains no inventory of assembled and machined parts; when a quantity of parts is needed, it is constructed from the ground up.

PRODUCTREPORT QUANTITY (number)

This command prints a product report showing, for each product, its unit cost when made in quantity "number." The report is spooled to an offline printer with a spool class of A.

WHEREUSED PART (number) LEVEL (level)

This command locates the parts that incorporate part "number" and lists them on the terminal. The list should be sorted with all duplicates removed. The LEVEL keyword provides some selectivity of the output. LEVEL(PRODUCT) locates only the products that incorporate the part. The IMMSUPER operand of the LEVEL keyword causes only the parts that are immediately superordinate to the specified part to be listed. The ALL operand of the LEVEL keyword locates all parts that incorporate the specified part (i.e., all superordinate parts).

WHATUSED PART (number) LEVEL (level)

This command locates the parts that are incorporated in part "number" and lists them on the terminal. The list should be sorted with all duplicates removed. LEVEL(LOWEST) specifies that only the lowest level parts (those with no subordinates) are to be located. LEVEL(IMMSUB) locates only those parts that are immediately subordinate to the specified part. LEVEL(ALL) locates all parts that are incorporated in (subordinate to) the specified part.

HYPOTHESIS NUMBER (number)

This command places the program in hypothesis mode. If "number" had been used previously, that previously defined hypothesis is used. If "number" had not been used previously, a new hypothesis with this number is started.

The use of a hypothesis simply means that DBO is concatenated to DBx, where x is "number." All read operations will first search DBx and then DBO if necessary. All write operations will be directed to DBx. Once the HYPOTHE-SIS command has been accepted, any or all of six HYPOTHESIS subcommands can be used.

END

This command terminates the costing program.

HYPOTHESIS Subcommands

DEFINEPART PART(number) TYPE(type) UNITCOST(cents)
MACHINING(machine,minutes) ASSEMBLY(line,minutes)
IMMSUB(part,quantity,part,quantity, . . .)

This command defines a hypothetical part (i.e., in DBx). The TYPE and PART keywords must always be specified. The type operand can be RAW, OUTSIDE, MACHINED, or ASSEMBLED. If the part is a raw material or outside part, the only other keyword that should be specified is UNITCOST. For assembled or machined parts, the only other two keywords that should be specified are IMMSUB and ASSEMBLY or MACHINING. IMMSUB defines the quantities of all parts that are directly included in the production of one part (the part being defined).

ALTERPART same keywords as DEFINEPART

This command modifies the definition of a hypothetical part. The only required keyword is PART. If the part is already in DBx, this command alters its definition. If the part is not in DBx but is in DBO, the part definition is read from DBO and the altered definition is placed in DBx.

The keywords are identical to those of DEFINEPART. If a keyword is not specified, no change is made to that characteristic of the part. If a keyword is specified, the corresponding characteristic of the part is entirely replaced with the information specified in the keyword's operand.

COMPUTECOST PART(number) QUANTITY(number)

Same as the previous COMPUTECOST command.

WHEREUSED PART(number) LEVEL(level)

Same as the previous WHEREUSED command.

WHATUSED PART(number) LEVEL(level)

Same as the previous WHATUSED command.

ENDHYPO

This command terminates the hypothesis command (removes the user from hypothesis mode).

Sample Terminal Session

```
PARTCOST
COMPUTECOST PART(3404) QUANTITY(1)
*** $18.44
COMPUTECOST PART(3404) QUANTITY(100)
*** $10.06
HYPOTHESIS NUMBER (6)
*** NEW HYPOTHESIS
ALTERPART PART(1206) UNITCOST(34)
COMPUTECOST PART(3404) QUANTITY(100)
*** $12.91
ENDHYPO
END
```

EXISTING MODULES

The following is a list of existing application program modules and operating system functions that are available for use by the costing system.

1. READ PART

IN—part number, list of data base names
OUT—part record, error code
If a list of more than one data base is passed to this and other functions, the data bases are logically concatenated for search operations. Also, opening or closing the data bases is unnecessary.

2. WRITE PART

IN—part number, part record, data base name
OUT—error code
If the part already exists in the data base, the error code is set and no action is performed.

3. ERASE PART

IN—part number, data base name
OUT—error code

4. FIND NEXT PRODUCT

IN—part number, list of data base names
OUT—part record, no-higher-product code, error code
This module returns the part record of the lowest-numbered product whose number is greater than the input part number. To find the first product, set the input part number to zero.

5. FIND IMMEDIATE SUPERORDINATE PARTS

IN—part number, list of data base names
OUT—list of part numbers, error code
This module returns a list of all parts that are immediately superordinate to the specified part.

6. READ MACHINE

IN—machine number
OUT—machine record, error code

7. READ ASSEMBLY LINE

IN—assembly-line number
OUT—assembly-line record, error code

8. GET-LINE

IN—nothing
OUT—next line from terminal, error code

9. PUT-LINE

IN—line to be written to terminal
OUT—error code

10. ALLOCATE PRINT FILE	IN—spool class, size of file OUT—file name, error code
11. OPEN FILE	IN—file name, type = read or write OUT—error code
12. CLOSE FILE	IN—file name OUT—error code If the file being closed is a print file, it is queued for printing on an offline printer.
13. PUT FILE	IN—record, file name OUT—error code

THE SOLUTION

The first step in designing the structure of the costing program is defining the function of the top module. The top module can be assigned the function "execute PARTCOST command."

The next step is viewing this function as a problem to be solved and choosing an appropriate decomposition method. If we start with STS decomposition, we might identify the problem structure as consisting of the processes: get next subcommand, parse it, execute it, and produce its output. The major input stream is easily identified (the stream of subcommands), but the output stream is not because the nature of the output stream is dependent upon the particular subcommand being executed. If we were careless and simply defined the output stream as "command output," we would undoubtedly end up with a module named "produce command output," a module which would have logical strength and an extremely complicated input interface.

This leads us to two alternatives, both of which produce the same result. One alternative is to modify the STS decomposition process so that the problem is broken into only two subproblems based on the point of highest abstraction of the input stream. This leads to two subordinate functions, defined approximately as "get next valid subcommand" and "execute a PARTCOST subcommand," and implies that the production of the output streams is pushed deeper into the program structure.

The other alternative is recognizing that "execute PARTCOST command" can be decomposed by transactional decomposition and, since this function obtains its input indirectly, it matches the model in Figure 9.2.

A key consideration at this point is distinguishing precisely between the functions "get next valid subcommand" and "execute a PARTCOST subcommand"; in particular, it is determining what is meant by a *valid* subcommand and what the interfaces will look like. Getting a valid subcommand could mean checking anything such as the grammatical structure of the subcommand, the validity of the subcommand name, the validity of the keywords, the operands, etc. The section in Chapter 6 that discusses additional factors of module independence gives us a clue on how to proceed. Ideally only one module each should have knowledge of the overall grammatical structure of the commands, the command names, and the keywords and operands of each command. Since it is easy to see that modules other than "get next valid subcommand" need to be aware of the subcommand names and the details of each subcommand, knowledge of the common grammatical structure of the subcommands will be hidden within this module. Hence, it will be named "get grammatically valid subcommand"; it will return any terminal input having the following form:

word word(chars,chars, . . .) word(. . .) . . .

The current status of the decomposition is shown in Figure 12.3. Module "get a grammatically valid subcommand" has three output arguments—the subcommand name, a yet-to-be-defined table containing the keywords and operands that appeared on the subcommand, and an error code (e.g., to indicate an inoperable terminal). Module "execute a PARTCOST subcommand" is decomposed by transactional decomposition. The interfaces show us that this module is the only module that is aware of the names of the six PARTCOST subcommands, therefore, it is the module that detects an invalid subcommand name. When such an error is detected, an error message must be written to the terminal, so a call was added to a "write message to user" module. Notice that the interface to this module implies that it is control coupled to its calling module because the input argument is a message number which the module presumably uses to index a table of messages. As was discussed in Chapter 5, this tradeoff is often desirable; it was deemed so in this program.

The interfaces to the six subcommand modules contain the operand table and a data base list (DB) which includes the name DBO. The modules must reference the parts data base, so they must either "know" that the data base is DBO or else receive it as an input. Because of some foresight that will be obvious later, the latter alternative was chosen. Because of some further foresight, the argument was defined as a *list* of data base names, although in interfaces 4–9 the list contains only one name. If we did not have this foresight at this time, it is likely that we would recognize the need for the data-base-list argument later and come back and make this change to interfaces 4–9.

One obvious question at this point is whether module "execute END subcommand" is really necessary since it does absolutely nothing. It was included in the design because its omission might lead to confusion. However, the module would probably be eliminated when the program reached the coding stage.

The next module to be decomposed is "get a grammatically valid subcommand." Its problem structure, data streams, and points of highest abstraction are shown in Figure 12.4. The first subproblem is satisfied by the operating system function GET-LINE. The second function is the module "parse a subcom-

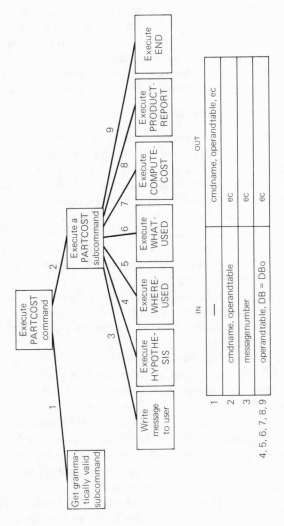

Figure 12.3   The initial decomposition

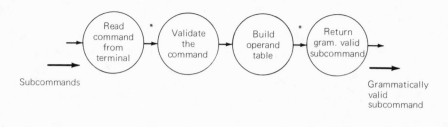

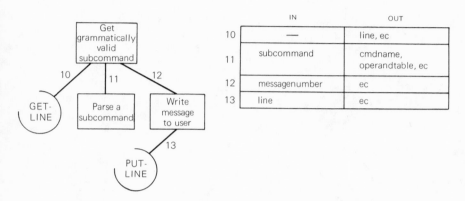

Figure 12.4   Decomposition of "get a grammatically valid subcommand"

mand"; given the terminal line as an input, it returns the subcommand name and the operand table, and it indicates whether the subcommand is grammatically correct. Hence, this module is the only module that is aware of the common grammar of the subcommands.

Since we are decomposing a source module that returns its output directly, the sink subproblem (returning a subcommand) appears in the logic of module "get a grammatically valid subcommand." In the event of a grammatically invalid subcommand, the user must be notified of the error and must reenter the subcommand. Therefore, a call was added to the previously defined error-message module.

Other than recognizing that "write message to user" needs to call the operating system function PUT-LINE, no further decomposition seems necessary here; accordingly, we can move back to Figure 12.3. The next module selected is "execute COMPUTECOST subcommand." Its problem structure is illustrated in Figure 12.5. However, rather than define a module with the specialized function "obtain PART and QUANTITY operands," the module was generalized because of the recognition that other modules (for other subcommands) will need analogous functions. Hence, one subordinate module is defined as "find an operand in operand table"; given the operand table and a keyword name (e.g., "QUANTITY") as input, it returns a list of that keyword's operands

111

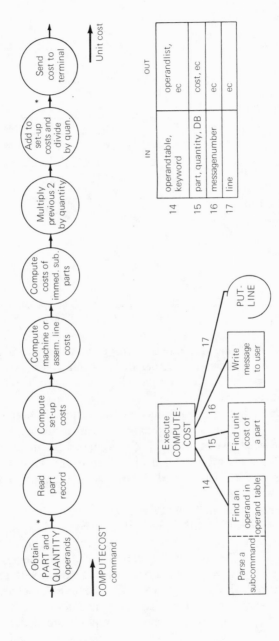

Figure 12.5 Decomposition of "execute COMPUTECOST subcommand"

Command: ALTERPART PART (7296) ASSEMBLY (997, 3)

Operand Table:

1	P A R T
0	7 2 9 6
1	A S S E M B L Y
0	9 9 7
0	3

Figure 12.6   A possible organization of the operand table

that appeared on the subcommand.* Since this module and module "parse a subcommand" are the only modules that appear to be sensitive to the organization of the operand table, they are packaged together as an informational-strength module. This implies that the definition of the operand table needs no further consideration during this design process; it will be defined when the informational-strength module is coded. (However, to clarify any confusion, a possible organization of the operand table is shown in Figure 12.6.)

The middle subproblem (the transform function) is described by the function "find unit cost of a part." Given a part number, a quantity, and a data base list, it calculates the per unit cost of the part when produced in the specified quantity. The last subproblem is satisfied by a call to the operating system PUT-LINE function. Because "execute COMPUTECOST subcommand" can encounter errors (e.g., missing PART keyword on a command, part not found in the data base), a call to the error-message module is also added.

Since the logic of module "find unit cost of a part" cannot be visualized easily, it is chosen as the next module for decomposition. The problem structure of this module is the middle subproblem of Figure 12.5. If the part is an assembled or machined part, the problem can be viewed as computing the following formula:

unit-cost = ((set-up costs for machine or line) +
quantity X (time-cost for machine or line
+ cost of the immediate-subordinate
parts))/quantity

If the part is an outside part or raw material, the formula is

unit-cost = unit-cost field in part record

The first formula is recursive (computing the cost of a part involves computing the costs of other parts) and the recursion is multidimensional, indicating that a recursive solution is desirable. Module "find unit cost of a part" is decomposed using functional decomposition as shown in Figure 12.7. The module first calls

*A *list* is returned because some keywords on some commands can have more than one operand, for example, the MACHINING keyword on the DEFINEPART subcommand.

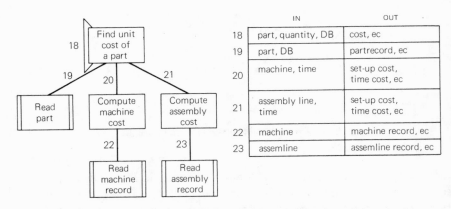

	IN	OUT
18	part, quantity, DB	cost, ec
19	part, DB	partrecord, ec
20	machine, time	set-up cost, time cost, ec
21	assembly line, time	set-up cost, time cost, ec
22	machine	machine record, ec
23	assemline	assemline record, ec

Figure 12.7   Functional decomposition of "find unit cost of a part"

Figure 12.8   Decomposition of "execute PRODUCTREPORT subcommand"

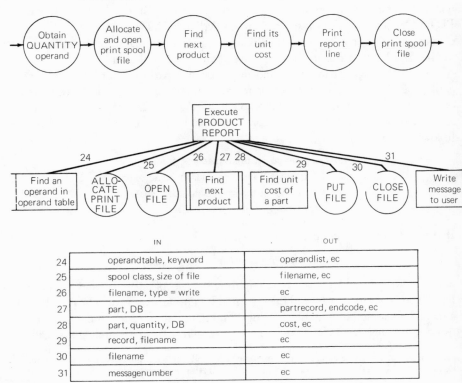

	IN	OUT
24	operandtable, keyword	operandlist, ec
25	spool class, size of file	filename, ec
26	filename, type = write	ec
27	part, DB	partrecord, endcode, ec
28	part, quantity, DB	cost, ec
29	record, filename	ec
30	filename	ec
31	messagenumber	ec

the preexisting "read part" module. If the part is seen to be a raw material or an outside part, the unit cost is extracted from the part record and the module returns. If the part is a machined or an assembled part, the manufacturing information is extracted from the part record and "compute machine cost" or "compute assembly cost" is called. These modules return the set-up cost and time cost for the machine or assembly line used. Module "find unit cost of a part" then iteratively calls itself once per immediate-subordinate part. When this loop of calling itself is completed, the module computes the formula above and returns.

The logic of modules "compute machine cost" and "compute assembly cost" is easily visualized, providing that they call upon the two preexisting modules to read machine records and assembly-line records.

The next module selected for decomposition is "execute PRODUCT-REPORT subcommand." Its problem structure is outlined in Figure 12.8. However, rather than formally decomposing this module, we can solve the problem largely from calls to operating system functions, preexisting modules, and modules already defined in the design, as shown in Figure 12.8. Notice that "execute PRODUCTREPORT subcommand" calls the module "find unit cost of a part" which was defined during the decomposition of "execute COM-PUTECOST subcommand."

Module "execute WHATUSED subcommand" is the next module to be decomposed. As shown in Figure 12.9, it was decomposed using a combination of STS and transactional decomposition; rather than having one transform function, it has three, one for each LEVEL operand. When module "find all what-used parts" is analyzed, it is apparent that this is a multidimensional recursive problem. Hence, the module is decomposed into a call upon itself plus a call to the just-defined "find immediate-subordinate parts" module. (Note that the logic for module "find all what-used parts" is essentially that of Figure 6.2.)

Module "find lowest what-used parts" is a similar recursive problem, and it is decomposed as shown in Figure 12.9. The logic for module "find immediate subordinate parts" is easily visualized, providing that it calls the preexisting "read part" module.

The next module to be decomposed is "execute WHEREUSED subcommand." The decomposition is similar to that done above. Three transform functions are defined (there is a preexisting module that performs one of these functions) as shown in Figure 12.10.

To decompose "find all where-used parts," we first see that it is another multidimensional recursive problem. Therefore, it decomposes to a call upon itself plus a call to "find immediate-superordinate parts." Module "find all where-used products" seems to be a similar recursive problem but we cannot solve it the same way since module "find immediate-superordinate parts" does not indicate which of the returned parts are products. Hence, we can view "find all where-used products" as finding all where-used parts and then, by referencing the parts data base, selecting the subset that is also products. The result of this is illustrated in Figure 12.11.

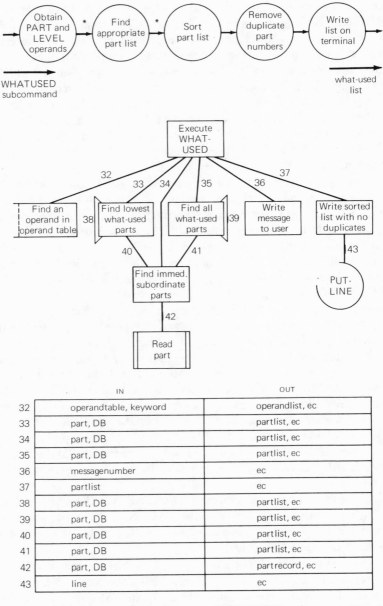

Figure 12.9 Decomposition of "execute WHATUSED subcommand" and its subordinate modules

	IN	OUT
32	operandtable, keyword	operandlist, ec
33	part, DB	partlist, ec
34	part, DB	partlist, ec
35	part, DB	partlist, ec
36	messagenumber	ec
37	partlist	ec
38	part, DB	partlist, ec
39	part, DB	partlist, ec
40	part, DB	partlist, ec
41	part, DB	partlist, ec
42	part, DB	partrecord, ec
43	line	ec

12. A Decomposition Example

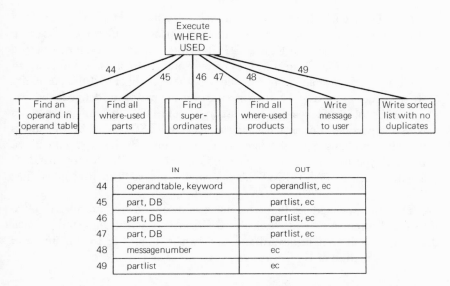

	IN	OUT
44	operandtable, keyword	operandlist, ec
45	part, DB	partlist, ec
46	part, DB	partlist, ec
47	part, DB	partlist, ec
48	messagenumber	ec
49	partlist	ec

Figure 12.10   Decomposition of "execute WHEREUSED subcommand"

Figure 12.11   Decomposition of "find all where-used parts" and "find all where-used products"

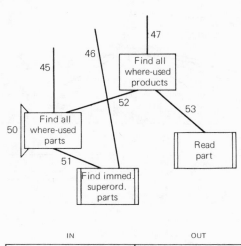

	IN	OUT
50	part, DB	partlist, ec
51	part, DB	partlist, ec
52	part, DB	partlist, ec
53	part, DB	partrecord, ec

The only module left for decomposition is "execute HYPOTHESIS subcommand." This problem appears to be almost identical to the problem "execute PARTCOST command" in Figure 12.3; therefore, we can decompose it in the same way as shown in Figure 12.12. (The only differences are a call to "find an operand in operand table" to obtain the hypothesis number and the possibility of writing an error message.) Note the reuse of many previously defined modules. Our foresight of including a data base list argument to the subcommand modules makes this possible. For instance, if the COMPUTECOST subcommand is entered in hypothesis mode, the data base list contains DBx, DBO; if it is entered outside of hypothesis mode (i.e., "execute COMPUTECOST subcommand" is called by "execute a PARTCOST subcommand"), the data base list contains just DBO.

The only two modules that have not been analyzed are "execute ALTER-PART subcommand" and "execute DEFINEPART subcommand." Their decomposition is straightforward and is shown in Figure 12.13. Figure 12.14 shows the structure of the entire program.

Figure 12.12   Decomposition of "execute HYPOTHESIS subcommand" and its subordinate "execute a HYPOTHESIS subsubcommand"

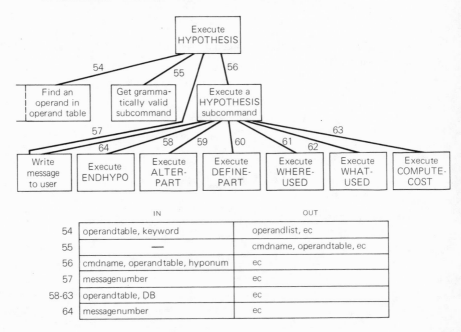

	IN	OUT
54	operandtable, keyword	operandlist, ec
55	—	cmdname, operandtable, ec
56	cmdname, operandtable, hyponum	ec
57	messagenumber	ec
58-63	operandtable, DB	ec
64	messagenumber	ec

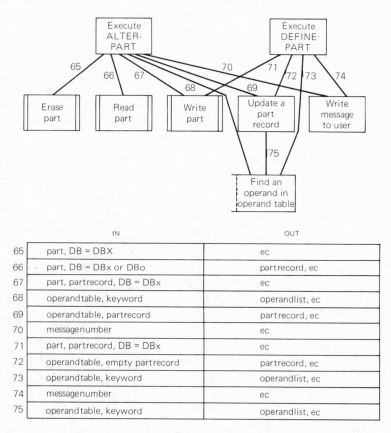

	IN	OUT
65	part, DB = DBX	ec
66	part, DB = DBx or DBo	partrecord, ec
67	part, partrecord, DB = DBx	ec
68	operandtable, keyword	operandlist, ec
69	operandtable, partrecord	partrecord, ec
70	messagenumber	ec
71	part, partrecord, DB = DBx	ec
72	operandtable, empty partrecord	partrecord, ec
73	operandtable, keyword	operandlist, ec
74	messagenumber	ec
75	operandtable, keyword	operandlist, ec

Figure 12.13   The final decomposition

ANALYSIS OF THE DESIGN

Although at first glance Figure 12.14 looks rather complicated, the program is not; the complexity of the diagram is largely due to the high fan-in of many modules. The program consists of 25 new modules. Of these modules, 24 have functional strength and the other has informational strength. The interfaces between the modules are rather simple.

In analyzing the coupling within the program, no occurrences of content, common, or external coupling are found. Ten modules are control coupled to module "write message to user," but, as was mentioned earlier, this was due to an explicit tradeoff. There is a small amount of stamp coupling via the part record in the data base. Seven modules are stamp coupled to one another because of

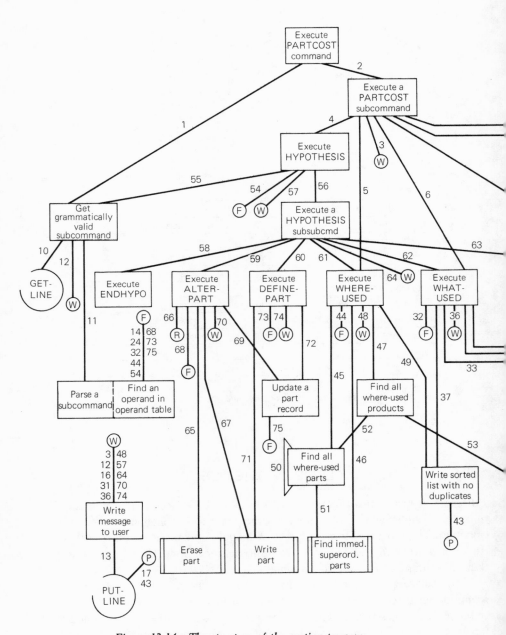

Figure 12.14   The structure of the costing program

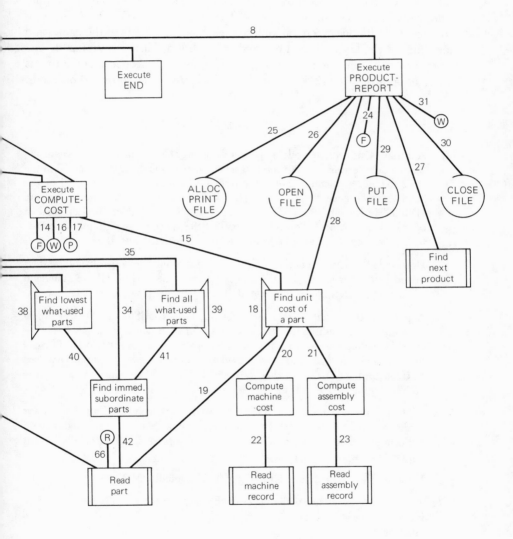

their sensitivity to the format of the part record. If desirable, this could be eliminated through the addition of another informational-strength module. This improvement is discussed in the next chapter.

In analyzing how knowledge of the terminal subcommands is distributed throughout the program, we can see that module "parse a subcommand" is the only module that is aware of the grammar of the subcommands. Module "execute a PARTCOST subcommand" is the only module that is aware of the names of the PARTCOST subcommands, and module "execute a HYPOTHESIS subsubcommand" is the only module aware of the names of the HYPOTHESIS subcommands. With one exception, only a single module is aware of the names and meanings of the keywords and operands of each individual subcommand. The exception is module "update a part record," which is a second module that is aware of both the ALTERPART and DEFINEPART keywords and operands.

EXERCISES

1. A mistake that is often made by people designing this program is not recognizing that module "execute HYPOTHESIS subcommand" should be decomposed in the same manner as module "execute PARTCOST command." That is, all of the "execute-subcommand" modules are placed on the same level, and module "execute HYPOTHESIS subcommand" has no subordinates other than "find operand in operand table". Module "execute HYPOTHESIS subcommand" simply adds DBx to the data base list. What are some problems associated with this?

2. How could the design in Figure 12.14 be changed to provide *nested* hypotheses? (A nested hypothesis means that the user could enter the HYPOTHESIS command while in hypothesis mode, thus concatenating more than two parts data bases.)

3. A mistake often made in implementing the WHEREUSED or WHATUSED subcommands is pushing the terminal-output function down to a lower level. For example, rather than writing the output from module "execute WHATUSED subcommand," module "find all what-used parts" is redefined as "write all what-used parts on terminal." This module calls the PUT-LINE function. What are the problems associated with this?

4. When module "execute PARTCOST command" was decomposed, a statement was made saying that if an immediate-subordinate module "produce command output" was defined, it would have logical strength and a complicated interface. Why? What ramifications would such a mistake have?

5. Is the preexisting module "find next product" unpredictable?

6. To become more familiar with the power of recursive modules, write the source code for one of the recursive modules (e.g., module "find lowest what-used parts" or "find unit cost of a part").

13

Optimization and Verification

After completing one or more decompositions of a program and defining the module interfaces, a common reaction is to briefly sigh with relief and then immediately proceed onward with the implementation of the program (i.e., precisely defining the interfaces and designing and coding the logic of each module). Experience has shown, however, that it is wise at this point to perform certain important reviews of the design before going any further. These reviews serve the purpose of optimizing or improving the design and verifying its quality and correctness. Spending a few hours or days at this point making significant improvements to the design and correcting design flaws will prove to be an invaluable investment over the lifetime of the program.

STRUCTURE OPTIMIZATION

The first step towards structural optimization is reviewing the design to ensure that the module independence in the program has been maximized as much as possible. The most important vehicle for doing this is the use of the informational-strength module. In other words, one should review the design looking for implicit or explicit assumptions and dependencies among modules, and then consider eliminating these dependencies through the appropriate application of informational-strength modules.

In the costing program designed in Chapter 12, we had the foresight during the design process to recognize that we should avoid making a substantial number of modules dependent upon the operand table. To do this we defined just two functions that reference the content of the operand table—the functions that build and search the table. Then these two functions were placed in an informational-strength module. This hid the concept of the operand table within a single module, thus making the definition of the operand table a decision that is internal to only this module.

If we review the design looking for other dependencies, it becomes apparent that seven modules are dependent upon the organization of the part record. Since the parts data base is also referenced by other programs, it is reasonable to expect that the content of the part record is volatile; that is, other fields might be added to the part record for the needs of other programs. At this point we have to examine the surrounding environment. If the preexisting modules that were used are part of a data base manager, and if the data base manager provides the concept of *data independence,* then perhaps no changes are necessary.*

However, since most data base managers do not provide data independence to this level of sophistication, we will assume that Hypotronics' data base software does not provide it; therefore, the fact that seven modules are aware of the format of the part record is a problem. A solution is to limit knowledge of the part record to only a single module by using the concept of the informational-strength module.

One approach would be simply packaging the seven modules into a single informational-strength module. However, since the seven functions of this module would be "execute ALTERPART subcommand," "execute DEFINEPART subcommand," "update a part record," "find all where-used products," "find immediate-subordinate parts," "find unit cost of a part," and "execute PRODUCTREPORT subcommand," such an informational-strength module is likely to lead to confusion. The reason for this is that the relationship among these seven functions is not immediately obvious.

A second and better approach is to carry the decomposition a little further by using functional decomposition; analyze the operations that these seven modules perform on the part record, remove these operations from the modules, and consolidate the operations in an informational-strength module. This strategy is illustrated in Figure 13.1.

In Figure 13.1, all of the functions that directly reference the part record have been consolidated in an eight entry-point module. Note that one of the original seven modules ("find immediate-subordinate parts") was absorbed into the informational-strength module. Another of the original seven modules ("update part record") was eliminated and replaced by two entry points in the informational-strength module. Figure 13.1 also shows the revised interface definitions. These definitions show that the part record is now only seen by the single new informational-strength module. This change reduces the number of new modules in the costing program from 25 to 24.

Another possible optimization is isolating all references to a particular file in a single informational-strength module. We have almost accomplished this in Figure 13.1 for the costing program; the only exception is the call from "execute ALTERPART subcommand" to module "erase part." An erase-part entry point was not included in Figure 13.1 because the part record does not appear in the

*Data independence means that each program can specify its desired logical view of the record. The logical views can differ from the physical representation of the record in the data base, and thus the physical definition of the record can be changed, for example adding new fields, without affecting existing programs.

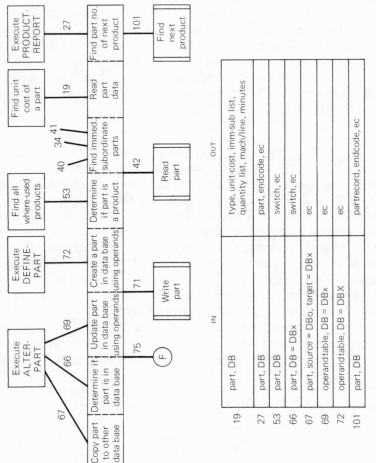

Figure 13.1   An informational-strength module that hides the part record

interface (i.e., no stamp coupling is introduced). However, if we decide that we want to accomplish both hiding the part record in a single module and consolidating all operations on the parts data base to a single module, then a ninth entry point named "erase a part record" could be included (and a call to pre-existing module "erase part" would be added to the informational-strength module).

The informational-strength module can be used for other optimizations, but most of these are particular to the program being designed and its surrounding environment; therefore, it is difficult to generalize the discussion. As an example, in the costing program, one might decide that it is desirable to isolate all interfaces to the host (operating) system's functions in a single module, thus making the program more portable (more easily transferred to a different host system). To accomplish this, an informational-strength module, such as that in Figure 13.2, might be defined.

STATIC DESIGN REVIEW

After any optimization alterations have been made, the last task is a review of the design to check its quality and correctness. The first step is a *static review* or *inspection* of the design. This step is simply an inspection of the completed design with respect to a set of criteria and questions. The second step is a *dynamic review* or *walkthrough*. This step involves establishing a set of test cases (typical external inputs and expected results) and mentally walking each test case through the structure of the program.

The static review can be an informal or formal inspection of the design. It is best done by having an independent observer ask certain key questions of the designer. It is important to note that the purpose of the review is to find weaknesses in the design, not to make any immediate "on-the-fly" improvements. The correction of discovered weaknesses should be deferred until after the review;

Figure 13.2 Isolating all invocations of system functions to a single module

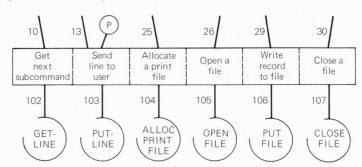

the psychological pressures present during the review can easily lead to hasty and ill-conceived decisions.

A reasonable set of questions to pose at a static review is the following:

1. Does each module have functional or informational strength? If any do not, why not? Note, as was discussed in Chapter 4, that there may be valid reasons for having an occasional lower-strength module. However, if this is the case, the designer should be expected to explain objectively how and why the tradeoffs were made.
2. Is each pair of modules either data coupled or not directly coupled? If any are not, why not?
3. Is the decomposition complete? That is, can the logic of each module be easily visualized?
4. Where a module or entry point has a fan-in greater than one (i.e., multiple immediate-superordinate modules), are the interface definitions to the module consistent? That is, does each interface to the module have the same number of input arguments and the same number of output arguments? Does each corresponding argument in each interface have the same attributes?
5. Is there any unnecessary redundancy in any interface? (Refer to Chapter 6.)
6. Are the interface data to each module consistent with the definition of the module's function?
7. Are there multiple modules in the program that seem to perform the same function?
8. Is each module described by its function rather than by its context or logic? Has each function been stated accurately?
9. Are there any preexisting modules that could have been used in this program?
10. Are there any restrictive modules (i.e., modules that are unnecessarily overspecialized)?
11. Are all modules predictable?
12. Are there instances where recursion either should have been used or should not have been used? If recursion is being used, does the proposed programming language support recursive modules?
13. Is there any aspect of the design that is precluded by the programming language to be used? (Refer to Chapter 14.)
14. Is the hierarchical structure too extreme (e.g., overly "short and fat" or "tall and lean")? Such extreme structures do not necessarily imply problems, but they should be explored because they could indicate that the decomposition processes were used incorrectly.
15. Has anything been left out? Are all functions in the external specification reflected in the program?

16. Has anything been included that should not be? Does the program do more than that stated in the external specification?
17. Is the design obscure? Does it contain anything that might be easily misunderstood?
18. Have any unstated assumptions been made?

DYNAMIC DESIGN REVIEW

The second review process is the dynamic review or walkthrough. This process begins by having someone develop a small set of test cases for the program. The program is then mentally "walked-through." That is, the program is "invoked" and the control flow among modules is mentally traced. When the program performs a read operation, the first test input is mentally fed to the program. When the program performs an output operation, the result of the operation is recorded (e.g., on paper or a blackboard).

Since the logic of the modules has not yet been designed, the participants must assume that the logic of each module is correct; that is, when a module is called, it correctly performs its function(s). During the mental execution of the design, the participants keep track of the internal state of the program (e.g.,

Figure 13.3 Initial data base contents

PART	UC	T	PF	IMMSOB	MACH	ASSEM
3333		M		3349, 1	47, 7	
4444		M		3349, 3	47, 12	
3349	.76	R				

MACH	SET-UP	PER-MIN
47	70.00	7.40

LINE	SET-UP	PER-MIN
22	623.00	24.00

DBo

DBM

DBA

interface data and file contents). The purpose of the review is to find errors in the design (e.g., missing or incomplete functions, erroneous interfaces, and incorrect results).

As an example, we can consider a few test cases that might be used to check the costing program design. One scenario of test case inputs might be defined as

```
PARTCOST
WHEREUSED PART(3349) LEVEL(ALL)
HYPOTHESIS NUMBER(1)
DEFINEPART PART(9999) TYPE(ASSEMBLED) ASSEMBLY(22,12)
          IMMSUB(3333,1,4444,2)
COMPUTECOST PART(9999) QUANTITY(50)
ENDHYPO
END
```

Since the costing program references several data bases, we must first establish a simple initial state of the data bases as shown in Figure 13.3. The PARTCOST

Figure 13.4 Data base contents as updated during the walkthrough

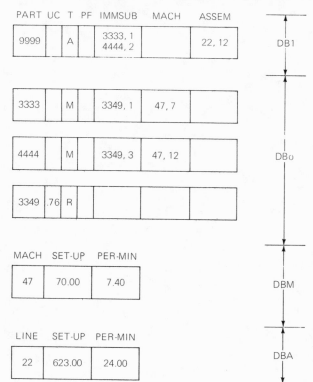

command would cause us to initiate the program and trace its intermodule control flow. When the first call is made to GET-LINE, the WHEREUSED command would be returned as output from GET-LINE, the command would be followed from module to module, and so on. Since the DEFINEPART command alters the state of the data bases, we would reflect the new part record in DB1 when a call is made to the "write part" module, as shown in Figure 13.4.

There are no general criteria available to indicate how many test cases to develop. As a minimum, there should be enough test cases to cause every module to be invoked at least once and several additional test cases that would represent unexpected and invalid-input conditions.

Although the above two review processes may seem either too simplistic or too time-consuming, experience has proven them to be invaluable. An investment of several hours or days during this phase of the development process is likely to uncover flaws that might have taken days or weeks to correct if left undetected until the later traditional program-testing stages.

14

Programming Languages

The methodology of composite design is concerned with the proper partitioning of a program into modules and the methods with which the modules communicate with one another. Since this type of structural design precedes the process of coding the program, the subject of programming languages has been largely ignored in the previous chapters. There are, however, some obvious relationships between composite design and the language in which the program will be encoded. Certain programming languages and language features aid or impede the application of composite design, and some recommendations in previous chapters are inapplicable to certain languages. The purpose of this chapter is to illustrate the strengths and weaknesses of the widely used programming languages with respect to the ideas of composite design.

Before analyzing the languages, a few additional definitions must be introduced. Most languages allow interface data to be referred to by different names in the calling and called modules, thus eliminating naming assumptions (a form of module interdependence) among modules. The name of an interface datum as known to the calling module is termed an *argument*. The name of an interface datum as known to the called module is termed a *parameter*. This terminology is often a source of confusion because, in some languages, arguments are referred to as *actual parameters* and parameters are referred to as *formal parameters* or *dummy arguments*. For consistency in this chapter, only the terms argument and parameter will be used.

LANGUAGE CHARACTERISTICS

To analyze the relationships between each programming language and composite design, a set of pertinent language characteristics is defined in this section. The languages will be analyzed in subsequent sections on the basis of these characteristics.

The obvious initial characteristic to be studied is whether the language

131

provides the concept of a module. That is, does the language contain a construct which exhibits certain characteristics: is it a closed subroutine, does it have the potential of being compiled separately, and can it be called from any other module in the program?

A second feature to take into account is that some languages provide a similar construct known as an *internal procedure* or *internal subroutine.* An internal procedure is a closed subroutine, but it cannot be compiled separately and it normally can only be called by the module in which it resides. Internal procedures are occasionally used as substitutes for modules when using composite design, but this is not recommended because internal procedures tend to have less-understandable interfaces. For instance, in some languages, arguments cannot be transmitted to internal procedures; in other languages, obscure *data scoping* rules exist. Data scoping is a significant consideration because it permits an internal procedure to directly access the variables in the enclosing module, a form of common or external coupling.

A third and important consideration in delineating the characteristics of a language is the argument-transmission method provided in the language. The four most common mechanisms are transmission by *reference, value, name,* and *value/result.* These mechanisms are of interest because they can restrict the means by which data are transmitted among modules.

Transmission-by-reference means that the *address* of the argument is transmitted to the called module. Hence, any reference in the called module to the parameter becomes a reference to the location of the argument in the calling module. Transmission-by-value means that the *value* of the argument is transmitted to the called module. In other words, the current value of the argument is assigned to the parameter, usually by copying the value of the argument into a temporary location and then transmitting the address of that location.

In the transmission-by-name mechanism, the *name* of the argument is transmitted to the called module. This can be viewed as the textual substitution of the name of the argument (or the characters in an argument expression) for all occurrences of the parameter in the called module. For example, if the arguments are X and Y+2 and the parameters are A and B, then all occurrences of A in the called module are replaced by the name X and all occurrences of B are replaced by the expression Y+2. Although this is the proper way to view the transmission-by-name mechanism, it is obviously not implemented in this fashion because modules are usually executed in their object code, rather than source code, representation. Compilers implement the transmission-by-name mechanism by compiling every reference to a parameter into a call upon a special subprogram that evaluates the address and/or value of the corresponding argument.

The last mechanism is transmission-by-value/result. This is similar in implementation to transmission-by-value, but similar in effect to transmission-by-reference. In other words, when the call is executed, the value of the argument is transmitted; however, when the called module returns to the calling module, the value of the parameter is copied into the location of the argument.

Not only does the choice of the transmission mechanism influence the way in which interfaces are designed, but it can also influence the behavior of the program. The exercises at the end of the chapter illustrate a program that produces four different results depending on which mechanism is used.

The fourth characteristic of interest is whether the language supports the concept of informational-strength modules.

Although the use of global data is contradictory to the ideas of composite design, a fifth characteristic to consider is the manner in which each language deals with global data. At the minimum, one should hope that the language should force a programmer to go out of his or her way to create global data; in other words, the default attribute of variables should be local rather than global.

Since appropriate application of recursive modules is encouraged when using composite design (e.g., the costing program in Chapter 12 uses recursion), the sixth consideration is whether the language provides the concept of recursion.

When a program contains some degree of stamp coupling (a group of modules are sensitive to the format of a non-global structure), and if for some reason it is decided that the stamp coupling should remain, then it is desirable to have a construct that allows the structure to be defined only once and then physically copied into the appropriate modules at compilation time. Hence, the presence of a compile-time macro facility to allow the definition of a data structure to be copied into modules is the seventh characteristic to be analyzed.

Given this set of language characteristics to consider, the languages to be analyzed in the following sections are PL/I, FORTRAN IV, COBOL, APL, RPG II, and BASIC. The ALGOL language was excluded because it is infrequently used outside of the academic world. The PASCAL language, because of its rise in popularity, might have been included, but it was not because the language definition is still evolving. Assembly languages were also excluded because they do not directly support nor disallow the seven characteristics. They give the programmer direct access to the machine; hence, an analysis based on the seven characteristics identified in the first part of this chapter would vary from program to program.

Language analyses are difficult because definitions of the languages vary from compiler to compiler. Even though standards have been developed for some of the languages (PL/I, COBOL, and FORTRAN), computer manufacturers' compilers often deviate from the standards in significant ways. The analyses in the following sections are based on prevalent inplementations of the languages, but they should be verified against the particular compilers in use in your organization.

PL/I

PL/I is a multipurpose language whose design draws heavily from concepts in FORTRAN, COBOL, and ALGOL. Although PL/I was once considered an "IBM language," compilers are now available from many computer manufacturers.

1. PL/I external procedures and external functions meet the definition of a module.
2. PL/I internal procedures and internal functions meet the definition of an internal procedure. Variables can be locally declared in internal procedures. If a variable is not explicitly declared, however, it refers to the variable of the same name that is found by searching outward through the static block structure of the module.
3. The default argument-transmission mechanism is transmission-by-reference. However, the mechanism can optionally be changed to transmission-by-value by enclosing the argument in an extra set of parentheses. The mechanism is also altered to transmission-by-value in a variety of other circumstances such as: when the argument is a constant or an expression containing operators, when an internal procedure is called and the attributes of an argument and corresponding parameter differ, and when a module is called and the attributes of an argument differ from those in an optional DECLARE ENTRY statement for the module.
4. PL/I modules can have multiple entry points and provide a mechanism for informational-strength modules.
5. PL/I allows a program to have global data; the name of a variable becomes global by specifying the EXTERNAL attribute in its declaration. PL/I data structures can be defined as global by this means (common coupling).
6. PL/I modules can be recursive. They must be explicitly identified as such by specifying RECURSIVE on the PROCEDURE statement.
7. The INCLUDE statement provides a compile-time facility for copying data definitions into modules.

FORTRAN

The FORTRAN language, perhaps the oldest "high-level" programming language, is widely used in scientific, numerical, and real-time applications.

1. FORTRAN subroutine and function subprograms meet the definition of a module.
2. FORTRAN has no concept of an internal procedure. (Strictly

speaking, the statement-function is an internal procedure, but it can consist of only one statement.)

3. The default argument-transmission mechanism is by value/result. The mechanism can be changed to transmission-by-reference by enclosing the parameter in slashes in the called module. (In many FORTRAN implementations, the default is transmission-by-reference.) When the argument is a constant or expression, most FORTRAN compilers transmit the argument by value. However, some do not; they allow, for instance, when the constant "2" is transmitted to a parameter J, the called module to inadvertently modify J. This modifies the value of the constant "2" in the calling module, a source of difficult-to-debug programming errors.

4. FORTRAN modules can have multiple entry points and provide a mechanism for informational-strength modules.

5. The COMMON statement defines global storage. There are two types of global (common) storage areas—blank and named. In a blank common area, the *names* of variables are not globally known. The global variables are placed in a single global block of storage and are referenced by their relative position. Hence, a global variable may be known by different names in different modules, a frequent source of confusion. If the COMMON statements in two modules are not coded identically in both modules (e.g., a variable is omitted from the list in one COMMON statement), the references to the global block of storage become inconsistent (e.g., a data reference in one module might reference the latter portion of one variable and the beginning of the next variable). This is another common source of errors.

   A FORTRAN program may also have multiple named common areas. Variables are placed in named blocks of storage. The names of these blocks are globally known, but variables within them are still referenced by their relative position. In comparing FORTRAN to PL/I, PL/I has no analog to the FORTRAN blank common area, but a PL/I variable or structure that is declared as EXTERNAL is analogous to a FORTRAN named common area.

6. Recursion is not permitted in FORTRAN.

7. The FORTRAN language has no compile-time copying facility, although some compilers have preprocessors that provide this function.

COBOL

The COBOL language, probably the most widely used programming language, is used extensively in business data processing applications.

1. The COBOL subprogram meets the definition of a module. However, the subprogram concept was absent from the original definition of the language and is not provided by all COBOL compilers.
2. The performed-paragraph is an internal procedure. However, no arguments may be passed to a performed-paragraph; this makes it a poor substitute for a module. The performed-paragraph cannot contain any local variables; all data references refer to variables in the enclosing module.
3. The argument-transmission mechanism in call statements to subprograms is transmission-by-reference.
4. COBOL modules can have multiple entry points, thus providing a mechanism for informational-strength modules.
5. There is no concept of global data among modules; the only provision for sharing data among modules is by passing arguments.
6. Recursion is not permitted in COBOL.
7. The COPY statement provides a compile-time facility for copying data definitions into modules.

APL

The orientation of APL language is toward interactive terminal environments and vector and array processing. Although originally thought of by many as a toy language for mathematicians, it is now used for sophisticated numerical and commercial applications.

1. The APL function meets the definition of a module.
2. APL has no concept of internal procedures.
3. The argument-transmission mechanism is transmission-by-value. APL presents some serious problems in this regard, the most serious being that it permits a maximum of only two input arguments and one output argument to a module. There are circumventions, but none are desirable. A set of variables can be packaged as a vector or array and then passed as a single argument, but this can be considered obscure programming style and it is not sufficient in many cases (e.g., when one wishes to return two outputs from a module—an array and a scalar variable). Another alternative is to define the interface data as global, which is also an undesirable choice. This restriction has been removed in at least one implementation of APL by allowing additional arguments to be transmitted

by name. Also, recent versions of APL permit the programmer to simulate the effect of transmission-by-name by using the execute operator.

4. APL modules cannot have multiple entry points, thus preventing the use of informational-strength modules.

5. APL has other weaknesses in its provision for global data. Any variable that is not explicitly listed in the function header becomes a global variable. Hence, the default attribute for variables is global, and this is a common source of programming errors. In APL, the term "global" has a slightly different meaning than its meaning in other languages. Global variables are not necessarily accessible by all modules; their scope is dynamic. When a global variable is referenced, the stack of currently suspended module activations is searched until a module is found in which the variable is declared as being local. The global variable now refers to this local variable. If the search does not encounter a module that contains this variable as a local variable, the variable is global to the entire program. In other words, the APL programmer can choose between making a variable truly global or just global to a module and all of its subordinate modules. Unfortunately, the programmer that makes this decision is the programmer of the *subordinate* module. As implied above, a "local" variable is not necessarily "local"; it may be global to some or all of the subordinate modules, and this cannot be determined without examining the subordinate modules.

6. APL modules can be recursive.

7. There is no "compile-time" facility for copying data definitions into modules.

RPG II

RPG and COBOL are probably the two most widely used programming languages. However, RPG is typically used to write rather small report-writing applications, and composite design is of limited value in such environments.

1. RPG does not provide the concept of a module; an RPG program consists of a single module.

2. The RPG subroutine is an internal procedure. No arguments may be passed to a subroutine. A subroutine cannot contain local variables; all data references in the subroutine refer to variables in the enclosing module (the program).

The remaining points about argument transmission, multiple entry points, global data, recursion, and compile-time copying are inapplicable because of the lack of the module concept.

BASIC

The BASIC language is typically used for the interactive solution of small engineering-like problems. Since most BASIC programs are relatively small and short-lived, composite design is of little use in this environment.

1. BASIC does not provide the concept of a module; a BASIC program consists of a single module. The CHAIN statement provides a way of linking programs together, but its effect is more like a "go to" than a call. The "calling program" terminates when it chains (passes execution) to the "called program."
2. The BASIC function and subroutine are internal procedures. The function receives arguments and returns a value, but the subroutine cannot have arguments. They also cannot contain local variables; all data references refer to variables in the enclosing module (the program).

Discussion of the remaining five points is inapplicable because of the lack of the module concept in BASIC.

LANGUAGE IMPROVEMENTS

Of the six languages surveyed, PL/I and FORTRAN seem most appropriate for use with composite design; however, COBOL is also suitable provided that COBOL subprograms (rather than performed paragraphs) are selected to represent modules. Although APL presents some problems, composite design can be used with programs written in this language. However, as noted in the preceeding analyses, composite design is of limited application in RPG and BASIC programs.

One can also examine the relationships between composite design and programming languages from another point of view: what features are *missing* in current languages that would enhance the use of composite design? A few such features are discussed here. The features will be illustrated as extensions to the PL/I language, although it is important to note that these features are applicable to any language.

One key problem is the realization that part of composite design is concerned with defining interfaces, in particular distinguishing between *input* data (data whose values at the time of module invocation have some significance) and *output* data (data whose values may be altered between the time of call and return). Unfortunately, this important distinction between data disappears in the source-code representation of the program. The difficulty is that a call statement such as

CALL FINDIMM (PART,STATUS,SUPPLIER,EC);

does not tell us which of the arguments are inputs and/or outputs of FINDIMM. This impedes our understanding of the program. If PART and STATUS are inputs and STATUS, SUPPLIER, and EC are outputs, then a more appropriate form of the call statement would be

CALL FINDIMM IN (PART,STATUS) OUT(STATUS,SUPPLIER,EC);

Not only does this aid our understanding of the effect of the call statement, but it provides the compiler with more opportunities to detect errors. Certain compilers perform a static analysis of the source program to find errors, such as instances where a variable's value is used before it is defined. Compilers cannot perform this analysis on argument and parameter variables because they have no way of knowing which arguments are altered by a call statement and which parameters have a defined initial value. This suggested change to the CALL statement and similar changes to the PROCEDURE and ENTRY statements would make this analysis possible.

The revised call statement provides another advantage. Arguments that are defined as inputs and not outputs (argument PART in the prior example) could be protected against alteration in the called module and its subordinates, thus providing earlier detection of certain types of programming errors.

We saw earlier that, in some languages, there are differences concerning which module (calling or called) selects the argument-transmission method. In PL/I it is the calling module that selects the mechanism, and in FORTRAN and ALGOL it is the called module that selects the mechanism. Furthermore, as discussed in the PL/I section, sometimes it is the *compiler* that selects the mechanism, "unbeknownst" to both the calling and called modules.

None of these situations is desirable because, if the calling and called modules make different assumptions about the transmission mechanism, the operation of the program is likely to be incorrect. Hence, in languages that provide multiple argument-transmission mechanisms, a desirable language improvement is one that requires both the calling and called modules to explicitly state the desired mechanism as an attribute of the arguments and parameters. The "linkage editor" or run-time environment could then check this attribute of each argument and corresponding parameter for consistency.

Another language improvement is associated with the use of informational-strength modules and the minimization of stamp coupling. Consider the costing program in Chapter 12 (Figure 12.14). An informational-strength module was defined to hide the organization of the operand table, but, to make the program reentrant, the operand table was transmitted through many modules of the program. The question is: how is the operand table declared in the modules that receive it as a parameter, pass it as an argument, but do not reference its contents? In PL/I we can consider three alternatives.

The first possible solution is to peer inside the informational-strength module to see how the operand table is declared (it would probably be a PL/I structure) and then copy this declaration into all of the modules that pass the operand table as an argument or parameter. Clearly this is unwise; it defeats the purpose of the informational-strength module and needlessly stamp-couples a large number of modules.

The second alternative is to realize that PL/I transmits arguments by reference (the *address* of the argument is transmitted). This means that the operand table could be declared as *anything* in the modules that transmit the table without being sensitive to its format. For instance module "execute COMPUTECOST subcommand" could be coded as

```
COMPCST: PROCEDURE(OPTABLE,DBLIST,EC);
DECLARE OPTABLE FIXED BINARY(15);
    . . .

    . . .
CALL FINDOPD(OPTABLE,KEYWORD,OPLIST,EC);
```

Clearly this has several disadvantages. Although it would work correctly, it is deceiving since OPTABLE is not a fixed-binary number. Also, if the compiler, linkage editor, or run-time environment was sophisticated enough to check the correspondences between attributes of arguments and parameters of external procedures (most current systems do not), then this alternative would fail (parameter OPTABLE in module FINDOPD would be declared differently, that is, with its true structure).

The third alternative, and probably the best in current PL/I implementations, is to declare OPTABLE as a pointer variable in all modules; the informational-strength module would then define the structure of the operand table as being based on this pointer. This alternative has a drawback shared with the previous alternatives: there is nothing to prevent one of the modules from inadvertently altering the value of variable OPTABLE, and this would lead to a difficult-to-debug error.

A better alternative is to define a new data type called a *name*. The *name* data type provides a method of passing a variable or data structure among modules without their knowing anything about its attributes or organization. A module that declares a variable as a name would not be permitted to alter the variable; the variable could only appear in CALL, PROCEDURE, and ENTRY statements. The DECLARE statement in the prior example would be changed to

```
DECLARE OPTABLE NAME;
```

Other possible language improvements are also associated with the use of informational-strength modules; for example, there should be barriers among the entry points in an informational-strength module. The hidden data structure should be accessible by all entry points, but other variables and parameters should be local to each entry point, and code connections among entry points (e.g., GO TOs) should be prohibited. This can be partially achieved in PL/I by enclosing the code for each entry point in a BEGIN block, but this has two drawbacks.

First, it adds additional execution overhead; second, the ENTRY statements cannot be placed within the blocks (meaning that each entry point cannot have its own private parameter names).

Entry points in an informational-strength module should be viewed as "peers," but in PL/I one of these must be arbitrarily designated as the "main" entry point (the procedure name), thus distorting the intended structure of the module. One can avoid this by beginning each function with an ENTRY statement and giving the module an arbitrary procedure name (and hoping that no other module accidentally calls this procedure name). A better solution is to define language constructs that allow an informational-strength module to have an arbitrary name (a name that cannot be called) and multiple peer entry points.

Although the use of global data is discouraged by composite design, global data may be occasionally necessary. In such instances, better language constructs could be devised to control its use. For example, each global variable should have an *owning module*. This module defines the other modules that are permitted access to the global variable and the types of access that are permitted (e.g., read-only). A linkage-editor (module binding) program could check the program for adherence. That is, when the linkage editor is resolving an external reference to a global variable, it could determine whether the owning module has permitted such a reference.

One last minor point of inconvenience is the restrictions that languages place on the naming of modules. For instance, IBM's implementations of PL/I restrict module names to seven characters (actually this restriction is not due to the language or compiler; it is a restriction of the underlying operating systems). In a large program one quickly exhausts the set of meaningful seven-character names (e.g., module "execute a PARTCOST subcommand" might end up with the cryptic name EXPCSUB).

EXERCISES

1. The following contrived program in a hypothetical language produces four different results depending on which argument-transmission method is defined for the language. What values are printed if the mechanism is transmission-by-reference?

```
DECLARE A GLOBAL
B=0
A=1
CALL ISUB(B,A,A+3)
PRINT A,B
END

ISUB PROCEDURE(X,Y,Z)
DECLARE A GLOBAL
Y=Y+1
```

$$A = A + Z$$
$$X = Y + A$$
END

2. What is printed if the mechanism is transmission-by-value?

3. What is printed if the mechanism is transmission-by-name?

4. What is printed if the mechanism is transmission-by-value/result?

5. When might the optional transmission-by-value mechanism, as in PL/I, be useful?

6. Under what circumstances would PL/I's changing the argument mechanism to transmission-by-value, as discussed earlier, be painful?

7. Some FORTRAN compilers transmit arguments by reference; others transmit them by value/result. Normally the effect is the same, but under what circumstances is it necessary to know which is used by your compiler?

8. If you use a language other than the six discussed earlier, analyze your language with respect to the seven factors discussed earlier in the chapter.

15

Relationships to Other Methodologies

The 1970s have been a significant and exciting time of revolutionary change in software development. Although the software field has obviously moved forward since the advent of digital computing, the pace of advancement was quickened in the 1970s. The 1960s, for instance, were a time when most of the software advances were concerned with understanding the *functions* of the programs being produced (e.g., advances in the understanding of operating systems and compilers). However, the technological advances of the 1970s took a different path; more emphasis was placed on the *methods* used to produce software.

During this period, software development ideas such as structured programming, stepwise refinement, programming teams, good programming style, top-down development, programming librarians, HIPO documentation, and code reading/walkthroughs/inspections have arisen, been refined, and been accepted by a large portion of the programming community. Because of the popularity of these techniques, it is worthwhile to determine how composite design relates to each in order to allow one to develop a coherent overall software development plan. The techniques will not be described in detail here because the professional literature abounds with discussions of the ideas. Myers, for one, describes all of these techniques and lists the key references in the computing literature.[1]

The relationships between composite design and HIPO (hierarchy plus input-process-output) diagrams will not be dealt with in this chapter because the subject has already been discussed in Chapter 2. The idea of programming librarians (paraprofessionals who perform some of the clerical tasks normally performed by programmers) also will not be discussed here because it has no apparent relationship to composite design. Likewise, the idea of formalizing code reading, walkthroughs, and inspections has no relationship to composite design although, as discussed in Chapter 13, design reviews and walkthroughs are an important follow-up to the use of composite design.

STRUCTURED PROGRAMMING

Given its popularity and the amount of literature on the subject, one would expect that structured programming would have a concise and universally agreed upon definition, but quite the opposite is the case. At one extreme it is used as a generic description of anything good under the sun in the field of software development, and, at the opposite extreme, structured programming is defined as simply coding without use of the GO TO statement.

Rather than defining structured programming as a concise set of rules, it is often better to speak of it as a spirit or attitude about structuring the source-code logic of a program: structured programming is the attitude of writing code with the goal of communicating with people rather than machines.[1] That is, the motivation behind structured programming is to produce code that is understandable by the human beings who will test, maintain, and modify the code, and to avoid the preoccupation of writing code to squeeze every excessive microsecond and storage word from execution on the underlying machine. This spirit can then be translated into six general, equally important, guidelines:

1. The source code is constructed from hierarchies of five basic program elements: single sequential statements, and DOWHILE (PERFORMUNTIL), DOUNTIL, IFTHENELSE, and CASE statements.
2. Use of the GO TO statement is avoided as much as possible. In particular, GO TO statements that jump *backwards* in the program's logic destroy the top-down readability property that is of key importance in structured programming.
3. The code is written using the guidelines of good programming style.[2]
4. The code is physically indented on the listing so that breaks in execution flow are easily seen (e.g., each DO statement is physically aligned with the statement ending the loop, THEN and ELSE clauses are vertically aligned).
5. Any sequence of statements, be it a DO-loop body, a code segment, or a module, has a single point of entry and a single point of exit.
6. Finally, and often overlooked, the logic should be a simple and straightforward solution to the problem.

As presented here, structured programming (and the related thought-process called stepwise refinement) is concerned with the design of the source-code logic of a program and is thus unrelated to composite design, which is concerned with designing the modular structure of the program. This observation is valid and means that structured programming and composite design are complementary. Composite design is used first to define the module hierarchy, the function of each module, and the module interfaces; structured programming may (and should) be used later when developing the logic of each module.

There are, however, two possible areas of confusion when applying composite design and structured programming together. The first is guideline 5, which might imply that informational-strength (multiple entry point) modules are inconsistent with structured programming. As was discussed in Chapter 4, this inconsistency does not exist; there should be no control-flow connections among the logic for each function in the informational-strength module. Each function has its own unique point of entry and point of exit: thus, the informational-strength module is consistent with both the theoretical and pragmatic views of structured programming.

A second possible point of conflict is the occasional suggestion (e.g., [3]) that structured programs be physically segmented (e.g., using the PL/I INCLUDE statement or COBOL COPY statement) so that each segment is small enough to fit on a single listing page. This could be interpreted as a form of "modularization" that might be inconsistent with the ideas of composite design. However, this conflict is not significant for two reasons. First, the idea itself is of dubious value because it interferes with the top-down readability property that is of vital significance in a structured program. Representing a PL/I module as a set of INCLUDE statements that name individual code segments appears to contribute nothing. This is because the INCLUDE statements do not specify the input and output data for the segments; thus, to understand how these segments interact to achieve the module's function, one must resort to reading the code for each segment. The second reason why the conflict is insignificant is that, if composite design is used, the modules should be small enough so that any internal segmentation is unnecessary.

PROGRAMMING TEAMS

Another recent, but somewhat more controversial, change in software development is an organizational change—that is, a recognition that programmers should work in formal teams rather than working in accordance with the traditional view of programming as a highly individualistic and private activity. The use of programming teams has been found to improve communication and education, encourage the idea of egoless programming[4], encourage the establishment of self-imposed quality goals, and maintain continuity when an individual unexpectedly leaves a project. Basically, there are three major forms of programming teams which are outlined below.

The *chief programmer team*[5] is headed by a senior-level professional and assisted by an equally capable back-up programmer. The chief programmer manages the team, performs most of the design tasks, codes the critical modules, and supervises the integration and testing of the program. Other team members typically perform the coding and testing of the individual modules within the program.

The *specialist team*[6] is also lead by a chief programmer, but in this case the chief programmer (in addition to the tasks mentioned above) writes all of the code for the program. Other team members have specialized assignments oriented to their particular talents. For instance, typical specialist-team members might include a back-up programmer (serving as a devil's advocate to the chief programmer), a documentation editor, a language and algorithm specialist, a testing specialist, and a person responsible for acquiring and/or developing necessary programming and testing tools.

The *democratic team* [4] has no formally appointed leader. It functions more as a committee where, during each development stage, the team member who is most qualified for that phase of development tends to become a temporary informal leader. Rather than having individual fixed specialities or specific formal assignments, the team makes its own work assignments based on the strengths and weaknesses of its members.

Besides the difference in leadership, another key distinction among these three approaches is the duration of time over which the team remains together. The make-up of the chief programmer team changes during the project; system analysts may be added for the analysis and design stages, and they may be replaced with "coders" (a derogatory term which I would rather not use) at a later point. The specialist team retains the same members for the entire project. The democratic team exists as a unit from project to project; that is, rather than bringing a team to a project (organizing a new team for each new project), the projects are brought to the existing teams.

Of these three organizations, the first two appear to be most compatible with the use of composite design. The reason for this is that composite design cannot be applied by a committee. The optimal number of people to use composite design to structure a program appears to be one or two. This is consistent with teams that contain a chief programmer. With such teams the chief programmer and the back-up programmer might apply composite design to the program, and then other team members become involved with the precise definition of all module interfaces and the design, coding, and testing of the logic of the individual modules. When composite design is used by a democratic team, no more than one or two persons should be directly involved in the design process. Of course, there is considerable work to occupy the other team members during this time, such as designing test cases, researching algorithms, establishing program libraries, and reviewing the design.

When composite design is applied by three or more people to a single program, the design usually suffers because, rather than tackling the design as one mind, the designers usually split the program into n pieces (where n is the number of people involved) and design each piece separately. This usually leads to inconsistent assumptions, inconsistent interfaces, and duplicated functions.

Although it appears to be necessary, if two people are designing the program, for the two people to work closely together as a single mind, an opposite approach has also been observed to be effective. In one case, two programmers using composite design to design an application program decided to work in total isolation for the first few days, each producing his own version of the design. They then exchanged their designs, studied each other's design to find its strengths and weaknesses, and then spent the last few days working closely together to produce a single new version of the design, incorporating the strengths and avoiding the pitfalls of the two previous versions.

TOP-DOWN DEVELOPMENT

Top-down development is unfortunately a misnamed idea; because it is concerned with the order in which a program's modules are integrated and tested, a more accurate name might be "top-down testing." In using top-down development, the first module to be coded and tested is the top module in the program. This immediately poses a problem, because the top module calls other modules; therefore, *stub modules* are written to simulate the functions of these modules. Once the top module has been tested, one of its immediate-subordinate modules is coded, the two modules are integrated together (e.g., link-edited) along with the necessary stubs, the combination is tested, and so forth. Although this form of testing has been highly publicized in recent years, it does present some subtle problems[1] (e.g., how test data is entered into the program and the problem of producing suitable stub modules), and a comparison of top-down testing with five other strategies has shown it to be deficient in terms of the thoroughness with which the program can be tested.[1]

Since top-down development is a *testing* strategy, it appears to be unrelated to composite design, and top-down testing and composite design have been successfully used together on projects. However, a caution is necessary. Some advocates of top-down development recommend that it can be overlapped with the design process; that is to say, that once the first few levels of the program's hierarchy are designed, coding and top-down testing of these levels can begin. From then on, the design of the remainder of the levels, and the coding and testing of the modules in those levels, can proceed almost in parallel. Although, at first glance, this might appear to be an efficient time-saving strategy, it is unwise for several reasons. One should realize that the use of composite design is often an iterative process. The designer might make alterations to the top levels of the design when completing the bottom levels, or, as was discussed earlier, he or she might complete the design and then realize that there is a better solution to the overall structure of the program, therefore, making a total redesign of the program desirable. Also, significant changes to the design are often made during the optimization stage (e.g., introducing informational-strength modules) and the static and dynamic design review processes.

This environment which allows change to the design must be encouraged (within limits, of course) because the improvements will significantly increase the adaptability and maintainability of the program throughout its lifetime. Problems arise, however, if the coding and testing of the program is overlapped with the design process. As soon as the first line of source code is written, a psychological barrier to any design improvements usually arises. Hence, if top-down development is being used with composite design, it is important to avoid the temptation of beginning the coding and testing before the design is finished. Furthermore, it should be cautioned that even though the design of the entire program has been completed, optimized, and carefully reviewed, top-down development still should not begin until one more step is completed.

THE NEXT DESIGN STEP

One last subject that is related to the use of composite design is the question of what happens once the program's structure has been designed, optimized and reviewed. That is, is the next step the design and coding of the logic of each module (perhaps with the use of structured programming and stepwise refinement) or are there one or more necessary intervening steps?

The question is answered by the manner in which module interfaces are defined by the use of composite design. The interface definitions are rather imprecise in that they describe the nature of the data being transmitted among modules, but they do not precisely define the attributes of the data. A typical interface description might state that the input is a part number and the outputs are a part-number list and an error code. However, it does not describe the size and type (e.g., character or integer) of a part number, whether the list is a linked or sequential list, what the error code means, and so on. Obviously the coding of the modules that share this interface cannot proceed until the interface description is refined to precise terms. Hence, a design step called *module interface design* must follow the use of composite design.

The purpose of module interface design is to produce, for each module, a *module interface specification* describing precisely the function and interface of the module. Although the design step itself is important, the formality of the step and the physical form of the specification are matters of individual taste and organizational standards.

The module interface specification should express all of the information needed to invoke this module from another module, *and nothing else*. It is important to note that information about the *logic* of the module (e.g., its algorithm and a description of the modules it calls) represents a separate set of decisions and should be excluded from the module interface specification. The information to be included is

1. The module or entry-point name. (Informational-strength modules have a separate specification for each entry point.)
2. The function of the module.
3. The number and order of the arguments.
4. The input arguments. This is a precise description of the meaning, format, size, attributes, units (e.g., radians, dollars, feet, meters), and valid domain (valid values) of each input argument.

5. The output arguments. This is a precise description of the meaning, format, size, attributes, units, and valid range of each output argument. Where applicable, the outputs should be expressed in a cause-and-effect manner to the inputs, that is, showing how the output values are related to the input values. The output of the module when the inputs are invalid should also be defined.

6. The external effects. If the module (or any of its subordinates) performs some action that is external to the system (e.g., input/output operations), these actions are defined in the specification. If any of the external effects are conditional (e.g., the writing of an error message), they should be expressed in a cause-and-effect manner to the inputs.

MODULE NAME: UNITCST

FUNCTION: FIND UNIT COST OF A PART. GIVEN A PART NUMBER, QUANTITY, AND PARTS DATA BASE LIST AS INPUTS, IT CALCULATES THE PER-UNIT COST OF THE PART WHEN PRODUCED IN THE SPECIFIED QUANTITY.

ARGUMENT LIST: CALL UNITCST(A1,A2,A3,A4,A5);

INPUTS:
 A1: PART NUMBER; CHARACTER(5).
 A2: QUANTITY; FIXED DECIMAL(7), MUST BE POSITIVE.
 A3: DATA BASE LIST; ONE-DIMENSIONAL ARRAY OF CHARACTER(4).

OUTPUTS:
 A4: UNIT COST; FIXED DECIMAL(7,2), UNITS ARE DOLLARS.CENTS, POSITIVE NUMBER.
 A5: ERROR CODE; FIXED DECIMAL(1).
  VALUE=0: UNIT COST COMPUTED SUCCESSFULLY
       1: A PART NOT FOUND IN DATA BASE
       2: PART DATA BASE I/O ERROR
       3: A MACHINE OR ASSEMBLY LINE NOT FOUND IN DATA BASE
       4: MACHINE OR ASSEMBLY-LINE DATA BASE I/O ERROR
       5: INPUT DATA ERROR (NEGATIVE QUANTITY, EMPTY DATA BASE LIST)
 IF VALUE IS NOT 0, A4 IS UNDEFINED.

EXTERNAL EFFECTS: READS FROM PARTS DATA BASES IN A3. READS FROM DBM AND/OR DBA AS NEEDED.

Figure 15.1   Module interface specification

149

Figure 15.1 is a module interface specification for the "find unit cost of a part" module in the costing program discussed in Chapter 12. The specification assumes that the program is to be coded in PL/I.

REFERENCES

1. G. J. Myers, *Software Reliability: Principles and Practices.* New York: Wiley-Interscience, 1976.

2. B. W. Kernighan and P. J. Plauger, *The Elements of Programming Style.* New York: McGraw-Hill, 1974.

3. J. D. Aron, *The Program Development Process: The Individual Programmer.* Reading, Mass.: Addison-Wesley, 1974.

4. G. M. Weinberg, *The Psychology of Computer Programming.* New York: Van Nostrand Reinhold, 1971.

5. F. T. Baker, "Chief Programmer Team Management of Production Programming," *IBM Systems Journal,* 11(1), 1972, 56–73.

6. F. P. Brooks, *The Mythical Man-Month: Essays on Software Engineering.* Reading, Mass.: Addison-Wesley, 1975.

16

Closing Thoughts

I have reserved this final chapter to discuss some of my personal opinions about the use of composite design and to answer some practical questions about its use.

To summarize the ideas of composite design, we can say that it consists of a set of concepts about program structure (e.g., partitioning, hierarchies, and module independence); a set of design guidelines, measurements, and goals (i.e., module strength and coupling and the guidelines in Chapter 6); a set of thought-processes (the decomposition techniques); and a notation for describing program structures. Composite design has many benefits, the two most significant probably being that the resultant program is easier to change in the future and easier to maintain. Other advantages usually seen are increased reliability (due to fewer design mistakes and a decrease in the difficulty of testing the program), lower development costs, and an increase in the probability of being able to use pieces of the program in future programs. All of these advantages add up to a reduction in an organization's overall programming costs, an increase in the probability of meeting schedules, and increased end-user satisfaction.

Since I consider myself a computer scientist, I should probably back these claims up with some hard numerical evidence, but I purposely will not do so. Given our current level of knowledge on software development, the surprisingly large number of variables that influence the outcome of a project, and the tremendous difficulty of performing meaningful software-development experiments, I put more faith in the qualitative feedback I get from experienced programmers than in quantitative statements such as "composite design increased our productivity from 197 to 278 statements per man-month."

I occasionally get such quantitative feedback, but, after quickly scanning it, I disregard it. I feel that it has no information content and can easily mislead others. What does 278 statements per man-month mean? What is and is not a statement? What is a man-month? What time periods were counted and not counted? What people in the organization contributed to the project in some small way but were not counted? How reliable was the program? How complex was the application? How intelligent and experienced were the programmers, systems analysts, test specialists, and managers? What other methodologies were used in the project? What are the users' opinions? And so on. Unless these and many other questions have been answered, and until their answers can be correlated, quantitative figures such as "278 statements per man-month" have less than no value (i.e., they are actually harmful because they can be misconstrued and can give us the impression that we know what we are talking about). Saying that "quantitatively comparing two programming projects is like comparing apples and oranges" is a gross understatement.

Although composite design has substantial benefits, the real gains appear in medium- to large-size programs, not, for instance, in the small and commonplace "master file update" programs. The largest and most critical use of composite design I know of so far is the development of an operating system, compiler, and a set of application programs for the launch processing system of NASA's Space Shuttle project.

PERFORMANCE

Probably the most frequent objection raised to the use of composite design is the feeling that it will produce slower programs. Since the issue of performance or efficiency is a complex one, we should explore its relationships to composite design from several angles.

The first way of examining the issue is to ask: although the use of composite design might result in a slower program (or on the other hand, perhaps even a faster one) than if the program was designed in some other way, how many of us should really care? If we make the assumption for the moment that the program will execute more slowly (this assumption is often incorrect) due to a greater execution frequency of call statements, we must ask ourselves if this is really important. For most programs (but, of course, there are exceptions), it is probably not that important. In most data processing organizations today, such factors as reliability, maintainability, and extensibility are more important objectives. What good is an online teller system with an average response time of two seconds rather than three seconds if the system fails every five hours, thus grinding the business to a halt? Even worse, what good is such a system if it intermittently processes a banking transaction incorrectly? What good is a fast application program in a Viking spacecraft doing experiments on the planet Mars if the program contains errors? What good is a fast econometric model if we cannot develop it in time to predict how to invest our funds for the next quarter? What good is a fast order-entry system if it takes us six months to change it to support a new terminal type?

Another way of looking at these relationships is to realize that most people are more interested in *computing throughput* (the amount of useful work done by a system over a period of time) than in the execution speed of the programs. Computing throughput is a function of the program's execution speed, reliability, maintainability, usability, and function. If the program is unreliable, the system's throughput drops. If the errors take an excessively long time to correct, then throughput is decreased because some or all of the work done by the system must be delayed until the errors are corrected. If the usability (human factors) of the system is poor, then throughput is reduced because of a higher frequency of user errors and longer human thought times in responding to the system. If the system's functions are insufficient, throughput is again reduced because work that should have been done by the system is placed on the user's shoulders.

If an existing program is too slow, another consideration is the realization that more speed can usually be bought for a price, but additional reliability, maintainability, and extensibility can rarely be purchased for an existing program. Speed can be purchased after the fact by such maneuvers as buying a faster processor, more memory, or faster communication lines. Unless the program is poorly designed, speed can also be purchased by monitoring the program, finding the traditional small fraction of the program that consumes the majority of the execution time, and then optimizing this part of the program.

Reliability, extensibility, and maintainability, however, can rarely be purchased after the fact. Additional testing and debugging efforts can lead to more reliability, but the costs are high and the payoffs are limited. Extensibility and maintainability are fundamentally related to the design of the program and usually cannot be improved without completely redesigning the program.

One way in which to directly explore the issue of whether the use of composite design results in slower programs is to analyze four factors that influence a program's efficiency. In conducting this analysis, each factor should be viewed in terms of the immediate effects (the effects right after the completion of the program's development) and the longer-range effects (the effects after the program has been placed in operation and has had the opportunity to be measured and tuned).

The immediate effects of the four factors will be analyzed first. The first factor to consider is *source-code efficiency,* the speed with which each module is executed, excluding the time taken by intermodule linkages (e.g., call statements). Normally we would expect composite design to have no effect on this factor. Surprisingly, however, composite design can have a positive effect on source-code efficiency, as indicated in Figure 16.1.

This relationship between composite design and source code efficiency has been demonstrated by a designer of IBM's PL/I Optimizing Compiler who has shown that the use of *small* modules can lead to improved source-code efficiency in programs compiled with this compiler.[1] The reason is that the compiler performs a significant amount of global (interstatement) optimization (e.g., intelligent register assignments and moving calculations out of loops), but the compiler must keep track of a significant amount of information to do this optimization, and there are upper limits on the amount of information it can manage. If the PL/I module contains more than a few hundred variable names, the global optimization cannot be done. If the module contains more than a few hundred

	Immediate effect	Longer range effect
Source code efficiency	0 or +	+
Execution overhead	– or 0	– or 0
Memory usage	+	+
Other resource usage	0	+

Figure 16.1   Effects of composite design on program efficiency

flow-units (a sequence of machine instructions that is entered only from the top and leaves only from the bottom), the optimization is not performed. This is a significant limiting factor on optimization because it is possible for a module with only a few hundred PL/I statements to exceed this limit. Moreover, if the module contains more than 4096 bytes of object code or 4096 bytes of data in automatic or static storage, extra registers must be used for storage addressing, and this reduces the effectiveness of register allocation optimization.

The study concluded by stating that the improvements in efficiency (from the compiler's optimizations) retained by writing small modules outweighs the cost of extra call statements. Although these remarks are based on a study of one particular compiler, it is likely that the phenomenon exists in other optimizing compilers.

A second factor in program efficiency is *execution overhead,* a measure of the overhead introduced by intermodule linkages. It is probably true that the use of composite design will lead to more frequent executions of call statements, which in turn will have a negative effect on this component of efficiency, but this is not necessarily true in all programs. Therefore, Figure 16.1 indicates a negative or zero immediate effect.

One often hears complaints about the overhead of call statements, but the complaints are rarely based on factual data. For example, COBOL programmers occasionally remark "How can you recommend the use of CALL statements rather than PERFORM statements when CALL statements take so much longer?" But when asked to quantify the difference in speed of a CALL and PERFORM, they usually have no answer. (The actual difference should be negligible.) Another example is that some PL/I programmers believe that calls to internal procedures are faster than calls to external procedures, a belief that is also incorrect. In addition, compiler writers and computer architects are becoming aware of the importance of program partitioning, and one is likely to see improvements in the efficiency of intermodule linkages in future systems. For instance, a module call in a program compiled with IBM's PL/I Optimizing Compiler is two to three times faster than with IBM's earlier PL/I F Compiler. The CALL/RETURN overhead in this newer compiler is the execution of only 29 machine instructions in most cases.

The third factor influencing efficiency is *memory usage,* and here the use of composite design has significant performance advantages. In a virtual-storage system, minimizing the working-set size of a program and the number of page faults incurred has a significant effect on performance. If the program consists of a large number of small modules, the modules can be physically ordered in virtual storage (e.g., by proper use of a linkage editor) in a way that minimizes paging. If the program is a large, monolithic, one-module program, the program cannot be intelligently organized in virtual storage without altering the program's code.

An earlier book explains a simple procedure to determine how to physically order modules in storage to minimize paging.[2] The program's design is studied to identify those module calls that are iterative and the probability of each module call (i.e., if module A contains a call to B, what is the probability that, when A is called, it will call B?). The placement of modules into pages is then identified in a priority order. The highest priority is to place two modules on the same storage page if one calls the other iteratively. The second priority is to place two modules on the same page if one calls the other and the probability of the call is high. The third priority is to study the common execution sequences of the program and to place modules that are executed in close sequence on the same page. If any modules still remain, the last priority is to attempt to place modules that are close to one another in the program's structure on the same page. An experiment using this procedure found that a program packaged this way incurred seven times fewer page faults than the same program with modules ordered randomly in storage.

Partitioning a program into small modules can have another positive effect on memory usage if the programming language is one that provides the concept of automatic storage (e.g., PL/I). If the local variables in a PL/I module are declared as automatic (and, in general, they should be to make the module predictable and reentrant), storage for them is dynamically allocated when the module is called and freed as it returns. Hence, a program of small modules will tend, at any time, to occupy less space than a monolithic program.

The last factor of efficiency is the use of other resources, for example, the length of time the program uses a tape drive, a file, a printer, a communications line, and so on. Composite design appears to have no immediate effect on this factor.

The longer-range effects noted in Figure 16.1 are based on the assumption that programs designed with composite design will be easier to change than if they were designed some other way. Since history has proven us to be poor at predicting the performance bottlenecks in the program being developed, a reasonable strategy is to avoid being overly preoccupied with performance during the development stages. Instead, develop a reliable and extensible version of the program, measure its performance to find the traditional 10 percent of the code that takes 90 percent of the execution time, and then, if necessary, optimize this part of the program. Since the use of composite design should significantly enhance the extensibility of the program, this after-the-fact tuning of the program should be more feasible; hence, composite design has a positive long-range effect on three of the four factors.

To summarize this complex issue, we are often guilty of overemphasizing program efficiency and neglecting to consider it with respect to the other, possibly more important, attributes of a good program. To a significant extent, efficiency can be added later to a program, but the other attributes cannot. Furthermore, there is no truth to the generalization that the use of composite design will produce slower programs; in fact, there is evidence that its use might result in faster programs.

PROGRAM MAINTENANCE

One could easily form the impression that only the programmers involved with the design of new programs need be aware of the ideas of composite design and that others, in particular maintenance programmers, need not be familiar with the ideas. Such an impression is wrong and easy to dispel.

A large portion of budgets for most data processing organizations is spent on program maintenance (defined here as fixing errors in, and making small enhancements to, production programs), implying that maintenance programmers make a substantial number of changes. Because the maintenance programmer typically works under a tremendous amount of pressure, there is an understandable tendency to make a "quick fix," that is, to amend the program in what appears at that time to be the most economical way possible. Such changes (e.g., adding a global data reference or weakening the strength of a module) can quickly undo the original well-designed structure of the program. Spier, for one, graphically illustrates how a program was reduced to shambles by a series of ill-conceived maintenance changes.[3]

If the programs being maintained were designed with composite design, and if the programs are being maintained by people who did not participate in the design of the programs, it is vital that these people (the maintenance programmers) thoroughly understand the ideas of composite design. Not only will they appreciate the programs' increased ease of maintenance, but once they understand the motivations behind the original designs, the maintenance programmers will themselves be motivated to alter the programs in a way that is consistent with the original design.

We can restate this as two key objectives for the maintenance programmer:

1. Have a global view of the program and a long-range view of the consequences of each change to lessen the chances of deteriorating the program's structure.
2. Modify the program in such a way that the resultant program has the appearance of being originally designed and coded that way.

PROGRAM MODIFICATION

Much of the program development (contrasted with program maintenance) done by data processing organizations involves extensive changes to existing systems and programs, rather than the development of entirely new systems and programs. Since composite design has been presented as applying to only the design of new programs, an obvious question is how, if at all, it can be applied to the modification of existing systems and programs.

If a system is being modified (a system is loosely defined here as a related collection of programs or a set of asynchronously executing subsystems) and the modification entails developing new, or rewriting existing, programs or subsystems, it is relatively easy to apply composite design in the process. However, if the modification entails changes to an existing program, composite design is usually inapplicable.

If the system being modified has some undesirable design characteristics, compromises must often be made when adding a new component to the system. As an example, an experimental attempt was made to redesign a part of IBM's OS/360 operating system by using composite design. The component selected was the OPEN function for sequential data sets. Because of the existing system design, however, the existing OPEN function was heavily common and stamp coupled to the remainder of the system. This was because of the sharing of a large number of control tables and data structures. Hence, all of the modules in the existing OPEN component were tightly coupled to literally thousands of other modules throughout the system, and redesigning this overall aspect of OS/360 was beyond the scope of the experiment.

The following compromise was made in the new version. The only coupling among modules of the new version was data coupling. However, since the OPEN function is required to obtain information from some of these system control tables and to build others, there had to be some sensitivity in the new version to these data structures, but it was decided to hide this in only one module—the top module of the new version. Hence, only one module in the new version was common and stamp coupled to the other modules in the OS/360 system. (This effort was just an experiment and was not incorporated in the OS/360 product.)

BEGINNING THE USE OF COMPOSITE DESIGN

The most significant problem in the initial use of composite design is the mastery of the substantial number of concepts, ideas, terminology, and guidelines associated with composite design. To contrast this with structured programming, a PL/I programmer, given a one-day course on structured programming, would leave with a sufficient grasp of the concept to begin using it the next day. This is not the case with composite design. The education process will take longer (and is best done a little at a time rather than being condensed into a few contiguous days), and it usually takes one usage of composite design on a program to get the concepts "under one's belt." For this reason, a course on the subject should include a realistic design problem, or the initial use of composite design should be on a noncrucial pilot project.

There is a significant amount of new and unfamiliar terminology associated with composite design, and this is another source of problems. To overcome this, avoid putting too much emphasis on the terminology at first; it is the concepts underlying the terminology, not the terminology itself, that are important. For instance it is more important to realize the disadvantages of global data than to memorize the definitions of common and external coupling. After using composite design for a while, the terminology tends to grow on you and become a useful communication vehicle.

Another mistake made in the initial use of composite design is to believe that it can be applied to all stages of design. Composite design is a method of designing *programs*, but, for instance, it does not directly apply to the design of *systems* (collections of programs). If one is faced with the problem of designing a manufacturing control system, one must first determine how this system is to be partitioned into individual programs; then composite design can be used to design each program. Although some of the ideas can be applied to system partitioning (e.g., maximizing the strength of each program and minimizing the coupling among programs), the decomposition techniques discussed earlier do not seem amenable to system partitioning. (There are, however, people who disagree with this and claim to have used STS decomposition to partition systems into programs.)

The use of composite design will quickly lead to a large inventory of modules, producing new management and control problems. For instance, one organization (an insurance company) that has been using composite design for several years has an inventory of over 13,000 modules. This makes the use of a program library system a necessity (there are many such systems available in the marketplace).

The organization alluded to above is making significant strides forward in the reuse of their module inventory in the production of new programs. Modules are documented and cross-referenced in four categories based on their probabilities of being reused.[4] The *local* category describes modules that have little chance of being reused. Modules in this category typically have high coupling, less than functional strength, and/or exist at the higher levels of a program's structure. Next on the scale is the *system* category. Modules in this group have both functional strength and stamp coupling and are generally only reusable in a specific type of application (e.g., premium billing). The third category is *global;* modules with this designation have both functional strength and data coupling and are estimated to have a good chance of being reused in a specific set of applications. Modules with functional strength and data coupling that seem to be applicable to many future applications are placed in the *utility* category. Such a classification scheme, plus the availability of a system allowing one to quickly peruse the inventory of existing modules, can significantly enhance the benefits of composite design.

Finally, remember that program design is still an arduous process. The use of composite design still requires, and is no substitute for, creativity, intelligence, and experience.

REFERENCES

1. G. Meacock, "PL/I and Program Efficiency," *Proceedings of the 38th Meeting of GUIDE International.* New York: GUIDE International Corp., 1974, 413–419.

2. G. J. Myers, *Reliable Software Through Composite Design.* New York: Petrocelli/ Charter, 1975.

3. M. J. Spier, "Software Malpractice—A Distasteful Experience," *Software—Practice and Experience,* 6 (3), 1976, 293–299.

4. L. Milligan, "Structured Programming—The After Effects," *Proceedings of the 42nd Meeting of GUIDE International.* New York: GUIDE International Corp., 1976, 601–612.

ANSWERS TO EXERCISES

CHAPTER 2

1. Where more than one call statement refers to the same module.

2. Usually none. However, it can occur in languages (e.g., PL/I) that provide the concept of an "entry variable." That is, the call statement refers to a variable, and module names can be dynamically assigned to this variable.

3. Yes. A recursive module (a module that calls itself or calls one of its superordinates) has this property.

6. The danger is that the module may sound more specialized than it actually is, thus reducing its possibility of being used elsewhere. For instance, the module one names "sort employee name table" might actually perform the more useful function "sort a single-field list." A module inaccurately labeled "compress teleprocessing message" might actually perform the more general function "squeeze redundant blanks from a character string." If one is interested in knowing a module's context, it should be apparent from the module's function and the input/output data along a particular interface.

7.

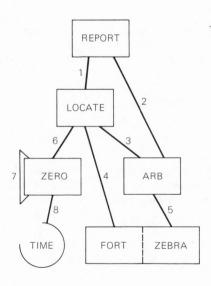

	IN	OUT
1	X	X
2	A	B
3	X	L
4	X	X
5	Z	Z
6	L	L
7	ALAN	ALAN
8	—	T

8. The fan-in is one; the fan-out is three.

9. LOCATE and REPORT

10. LOCATE and ARB

11. Nothing. It is ambiguous.

CHAPTER 4

3a. Communicational

3b. Logical

3c. Functional

3d. Communicational

3e. Functional

3f. Logical

3g. Informational

3h. Functional

3i. Classical

3j. Communicational

3k. Procedural

3l. Coincidental

3m. Functional

3n. Coincidental (Not logical strength; the functions appear to be unrelated.)

3o. Functional (All modules probably test for exceptional and error situations.)

3p. Informational

3q. Coincidental (Not a class of related functions.)

3r. Functional

3s. Procedural

3t. Cannot be determined. "Mainline control module" is a description of *logic*, but analysis of module strength requires examination of *function*. This module might have any of the categories of strength, but we cannot determine which without knowing its function.

3u. Classical

3v. Coincidental (Multiple entry points do not necessarily imply an informational-strength module.)

CHAPTER 5

1. The major problem is control coupling, since finding all occurrences of it requires one to determine if a sending module perceives a piece of interface data as control information. A second problem occurs with arrays: determining whether their elements have a homogeneous or heterogeneous meaning.

2.

A-B: data	B-D: data	C-G: none
A-C: external	B-E: control	D-E: none
A-D: none	B-F: stamp*	D-F: none
A-E: none	B-G: none	D-G: data
A-F: common	C-D: data	E-F: stamp*
A-G: common	C-E: none	E-G: none
B-C: none	C-F: none	F-G: common

   *A reasonable assumption, but we cannot tell for sure without looking inside modules B, E, and F to see if they are aware of the format of the record.

3. Module A or F. Both are coupled to four other modules and the coupling is tight. A's four couplings are data, external, common, and common. F's are stamp, stamp, common, and common.

4. Yes, but this chapter discusses only direct coupling. For instance, if module X is data coupled to Y and Y is data coupled to Z, we could say that there is a "second-order" form of coupling between X and Z. However, considerations of such "nth-order" couplings quickly explode into a massive combinatorial problem, making them of no known use today in the design process. This issue of higher-order, indirect forms of coupling is explored in a mathematical sense in Chapter 10 of G. J. Myers, *Reliable Software Through Composite Design.* New York: Petrocelli/Charter, 1975.

CHAPTER 6

1. Although one effect of partitioning is the reduction of the number of simultaneous concepts that the programmer or designer must comprehend, an *excessive* number of module interfaces can have the opposite effect. Hence, the average module size should be roughly equal to the square root of the estimated number of executable statements in the program.

2. The concept of counting valid and invalid records is not an integral part of the function of editing a record. The module is less independent than need be because it is aware of this concept and of the attributes (e.g., size, representation) of the counter variables.

3. Absolutely not. The error code is pertinent to the module's function.

4. Not really. Its function is predictable; each invocation of the module causes its function to be performed exactly as stated.

5. a,d—no. b,c,e—yes.

6. FORTRAN, COBOL, RPG–no.
   PL/I, APL, ALGOL–yes.
   Assembly languages—yes, but you must create the necessary mechanisms.

CHAPTER 8

1. The function of the top module is: add scouting reports to scouting file and produce scouting attention report. (Communicational strength)

2.

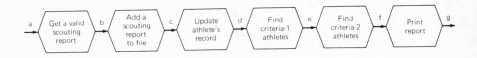

3. Major input stream: scouting reports
   Major output stream: scouting attention report

4. The first point is b. The second point is d (at this point all of the requisite data exists in the file).

5. The three modules are:
   1. Get a valid scouting report
   2. Update scouting file with scouting report
   3. Produce scouting attention report
   The interfaces are:

IN	OUT
1: nothing	scouting report, end-of-input flag, error-code
2: scouting report	error-code
3: nothing	error-code

6. The problem structures are shown below. Points of highest abstraction are marked with an asterisk.

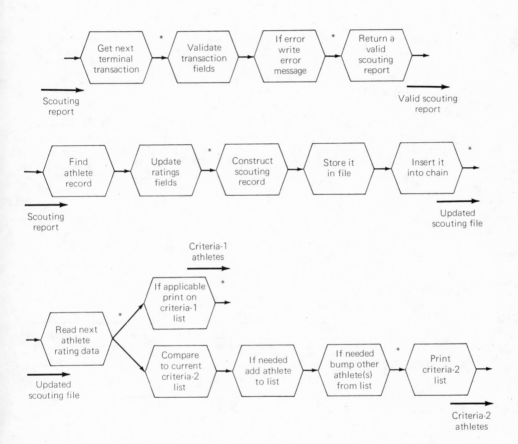

7. One reasonable solution is shown below. If your solution is different, compare it to the solution below and convince yourself why your design is better or worse.

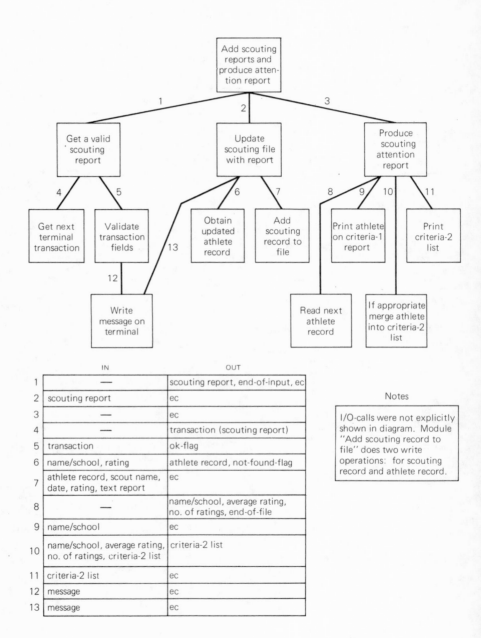

	IN	OUT
1	—	scouting report, end-of-input, ec
2	scouting report	ec
3	—	ec
4	—	transaction (scouting report)
5	transaction	ok-flag
6	name/school, rating	athlete record, not-found-flag
7	athlete record, scout name, date, rating, text report	ec
8	—	name/school, average rating, no. of ratings, end-of-file
9	name/school	ec
10	name/school, average rating, no. of ratings, criteria-2 list	criteria-2 list
11	criteria-2 list	ec
12	message	ec
13	message	ec

Notes

I/O-calls were not explicitly shown in diagram. Module "Add scouting record to file" does two write operations: for scouting record and athlete record.

166

8. There are four: scouting report, athlete record, scouting record, and criteria-2 list (a two-field-per-entry list).

9. Modules "validate transaction fields" and "update scouting file with report" are stamp coupled because they are sensitive to the format of the scouting report. Modules "obtain updated athlete record," "add scouting record to file," and "read next athlete record" are stamp coupled via the athlete record. The scouting record introduces no stamp coupling. Modules "if appropriate merge athlete into criteria-2 list" and "print criteria-2 list" are stamp coupled because of common knowledge of the criteria-2 list. Note that any or all of these occurrences of stamp coupling could be eliminated by creating the appropriate informational-strength modules.

CHAPTER 9

1. b, c, e, and f.

CHAPTER 10

1. Because it contains a distinct idea. Adding this material to Chapter 9 would have resulted in a "classical-strength chapter."

2. The module references the athlete record to obtain the pointer of the first scouting record. It later places the pointer to the new scouting record in this field and writes the athlete record back to the file. Two subordinate functions could be defined as "get address of first scouting record from athlete record" and "rewrite athlete record with new scouting record chain pointer." These functions could then be combined with the two other modules that are sensitive to the athlete record to form a four-function, informational-strength module that hides the organization of the athlete record from the rest of the program. This revision to the program is shown in the following diagram.

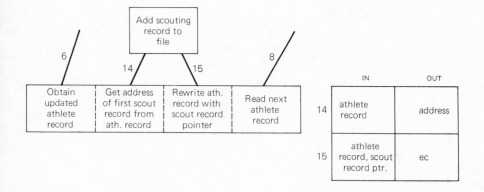

ANSWERS TO EXERCISES

CHAPTER 12

1. It makes module "execute a PARTCOST subcommand" more complex, since it would have to determine whether the data base list has one or two entries to determine whether a subcommand is valid or not (i.e., determining whether or not the user is in hypothesis mode). Also, since the data base list would probably exist as static storage in this module, the module is unpredictable and the program is nonreentrant (meaning that one physical copy of the program could not serve multiple terminal users).

2. The change is simple: just add a call from module "execute a HYPOTHESIS subsubcommand" to module "execute HYPOTHESIS subcommand" (another use of recursion). Note that if the mistake in excercise 1 had been made, this extension would be much more difficult.

3. Placing the output function within or subordinate to the recursive modules would preclude formating and sorting the output, since the output would be written "on the fly." Also such a change would make the recursive modules less reusable (HYPO-TRONICS is likely to have other programs needing these bill-of-material implosion and explosion functions).

4. The module would have logical strength because it would perform a class of related (i.e., outputting) functions, where one of the functions is explicitly selected by its calling module for each invocation. The module would receive a function code selecting among the functions "print product/cost list," "write part list on terminal," and "write unit cost on terminal." The interface would be complicated because it would have to contain a product and cost list, a part list, and a cost argument. Since this information would have to be returned through many lower-level modules, many other interfaces would be equally complicated. Also, either the lower-level modules would return this function code (leading to considerable control coupling) or module "execute PARTCOST command" would have to be aware of the semantics of the subcommands. Furthermore, the introduction of new functions (e.g., subcommands) to the program would undoubtedly ripple into this module and many of the intervening modules. In short, such a mistake would have a devastating effect on the program.

5. No. It has no memory from one call to another. If it had been defined without its part-number input argument (meaning that it would have to "remember" where to continue from), then it would be an unpredictable module.

CHAPTER 14

1. A=6, B=12
2. A=5, B=0
3. A=7, B=14
4. A=2, B=7

5. If a module wishes to pass an input argument to a subordinate module and protect the argument from modification.

6. If the argument is an output argument, its value will be unchanged when the called module returns and the problem will be difficult to diagnose.

7. One circumstance is when the called module "blows up" and the system unfortunately presents the programmer with only a storage dump. If the programmer attempts to find out where the called module terminated by examining the value of the arguments in the dump, he will be misled if the mechanism is value/result.

INDEX